War in My Town

War in My Town

E. GRAZIANI

Second Story Press

Library and Archives Canada Cataloguing in Publication

Graziani, E., 1961-, author
War in my town / by E. Graziani.

Issued in print and electronic formats.
ISBN 978-1-927583-71-5 (pbk.).—ISBN 978-1-927583-72-2 (epub)

1. World War, 1939-1945—Italy—Juvenile fiction. I. Title.

PS8613.R395W37 2015   jC813'.6   C2014-908151-0

C2014-908152-9

Managing editor: Carolyn Jackson
Editor: Sarah Swartz
Designer: Melissa Kaita
Cover photographs © iStockphoto and Shutterstock

Printed and bound in Canada

Second Story Press gratefully acknowledges the support of the Ontario Arts Council and the Canada Council for the Arts for our publishing program. We acknowledge the financial support of the Government of Canada through the Canada Book Fund.

ONTARIO ARTS COUNCIL
CONSEIL DES ARTS DE L'ONTARIO
an Ontario government agency
un organisme du gouvernement de l'Ontario

Canada Council
for the Arts

Conseil des Arts
du Canada

Published by
Second Story Press
20 Maud Street, Suite 401
Toronto, ON M5V 2M5
www.secondstorypress.ca

ↄ⟨

*This book is dedicated to my mother and father,
Bruna and Edo, and their families.*

*To the people of Eglio and Sassi in Garfagnana,
Tuscany, Italy — may they never forget.*

*To my husband, Nanni, for his patience and understanding.
And to my daughters, Julia, Alicia, Michaila, and Chiara,
for sharing me with the written word.*

ↄ⟨

Preface

This book is based on the personal accounts of my mother, Bruna Pucci Guazzelli, and father, Edo Guazzelli. The events in Eglio (pronounced el-i-o, with a silent "g"), a village in northern Tuscany, occurred during World War II, between the spring of 1940 and the spring of 1945. But it is important to understand a few things before the story is told.

I am a first generation Italian Canadian. I was born, educated, and raised in Canada. In addition to having been blessed by my parents' decision to immigrate here in 1958, there were also many advantages to being raised in an Italian household. First of all the food was great. Second, I could always count on boisterous family gatherings in which cousins, aunts, uncles, friends, and *paesani* (fellow villagers) were unconditionally welcomed and expected. Third, our Italian culture and history was a regular topic at the dinner table, and both my brother and I listened respectfully to the stories my mother and my father proudly shared about their younger years. Listening to them as a child, their stories fascinated me. As a teen, I admit they were a little annoying. As an adult, I began to appreciate them. Today, I am grateful to have heard these accounts and to know where my parents came from.

The stories that stayed with me were the old retellings of events that took place in their Northern Tuscany village during World War II. These narratives, as with most things in life, range from the tragic and the appalling to the awe-inspiring. Tragic, because war means killing the "enemy." The enemy is always a group of individuals: men, women and children, the elderly, and the infirm. Appalling, because of the cold-hearted, systematic, and merciless campaign of Jewish genocide that began in 1933 Nazi Germany under Chancellor Adolf Hitler and resulted in the murder of some six million innocent people by the war's end in 1945.

We know why World War II was tragic and appalling, but why awe-inspiring? I think because of the triumph of the human spirit and the power of the will to live. It is a testament to the resilience and resourcefulness of people and the power of love for family and friends, staying together to overcome the upheaval of war and becoming all the stronger. It is a tribute to the unselfish willingness of people to assist one another in times of profound adversity. It is a witness to small everyday miracles, such as a young girl growing into womanhood despite the turmoil surrounding her.

What happened in my mother and father's native Italian village during the Nazi occupation was not unique. There must have been millions of similar stories. What made them so special to Bruna and Edo was the fact that retelling these events kept the people who perished alive — for them and for the next generation. Their essence and spirit lived on in my parents' memories. We still feel them near us when we speak of them, kindly and lovingly.

For this reason, I am retelling my mother's memories. None of the people I have written about are fictitious. They are one hundred percent real. The events that took place in the village of Eglio before and during the Battle of Garfagnana on the Gothic Line in the last days of World War II need to be told. My mother claimed that sometimes, when we only look at the big picture, we lose sight of the important little things. She was right. Though I studied wars from the Dark Ages through to the First and Second World Wars at university as a history major, I rarely focused on the people, the individuals who suffered and died, and the lives that were lost. For each death, in each war, there was a family shattered, a lifetime of wonder stolen, dreams unfulfilled, future generations unrealized, a story incomplete. Humanity should not lose sight of this fact.

My mother's story starts on the eve of Mussolini's declaration of war on France and Britain in 1940. But war in Europe had begun long before that and although this is a story of an Italian village and the common people victimized by Nazi soldiers, not all Italians were victims. Italy was a fascist nation, allied with Germany as one of the Axis nations. Initially, racism and anti-Semitism was not a part of Italian fascism, though it was part of Nazi fascism. Unlike Hitler, Mussolini was not as interested in genocide. But eventually, Mussolini adopted these terrible racist policies, too.

Adolf Hitler and his followers believed that they were the so-called "superior" Aryan race, and that all "inferior" people, such as Jews, Roma (gypsies), and disabled people, should be killed. Within Germany, the Nazis began waging a war on the Jewish people by creating unfair laws, and restricting their freedom. At first, Jewish people and other non-Aryans were not allowed to practice law or work in the civil service, to become journalists, or own land. All Jews had to wear stars and Jewish children were no longer allowed to go to school. Later the laws became more deadly. The Nazis established the first concentration camp for Jews in Dachau in 1933, and by 1945 that number would grow to more than one thousand camps, throughout Europe. As Germany invaded other nations, these laws became the laws of those countries, too.

Under Benito Mussolini, Italy joined forces with Nazi Germany. After becoming increasingly disenchanted with their leader, the Italian people revolted against him and put him in prison. Under a new leader, all of Italy surrendered to the Allied nations at that time — Great Britain, Canada, the United States, Russia and the opposing French Forces — from July to September, 1943. But soon after, the Nazis captured and occupied Central and Northern Italy including Tuscany — where this story takes place. Mussolini was freed and again came into power in this part of Italy under Nazi Germany. On October 13, 1943, one month after Italy surrendered to Allied forces, it declared war on Nazi Germany, its onetime Axis partner.

Now the battles between the fascist Axis and the Allies were heightened and in 1945, the "Gothic Line" was one of the last European fronts in World War II. The Gothic Line passed through the Garfagnana region in Northern Tuscany, where my mother's village of Eglio is located.

Eglio in the Garfanana area of Tuscany.
Poggetti, the family home, is the darker
house at the lower far right.

My hope is that in passing on her memories, the people my mother recalls will not be lost. Maybe her little corner of the world and the everyday heroes who still inhabit her stories will live on in others.

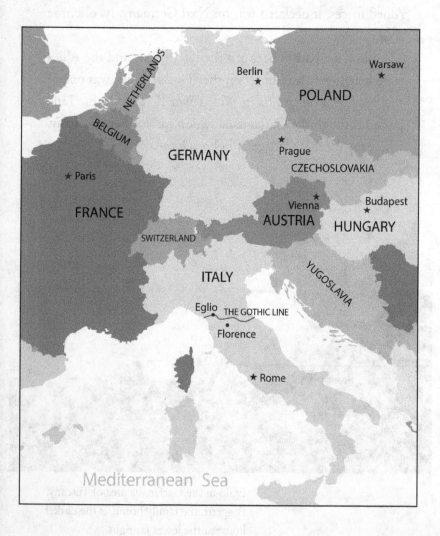

PART ONE

Italy Before the War

Benito Mussolini, or *Il Duce* (the "Duke," in Italian) as he was called, first rose to power in Italy in the 1920s. After World War I, there was much unemployment, poverty and bitterness amongst the Italian people. Amidst the suffering, Mussolini made promises of a better life to the workers, farmers, and businessmen. He was a strong speaker and he took advantage of the chaos in Italy at this time. Though he was elected by the people, once he was in power Mussolini became a brutal dictator, took control of the army and enacted laws so that no one could speak against him or oppose him. He created the Fascist Party.

This was the beginning of fascism. The Italian word *fascio* — meaning a bundle — is a symbol of strength through unity and the image of an axe in a bundle of rods became the emblem of the Fascist Party. Under Mussolini the party combined violence and bullying to gain control of the Italian government. Critics of Mussolini were beaten up by his supporters, the Blackshirts. Newspapers that didn't support him were shut down, and political rivals who criticized him were intimidated by his armed Blackshirts. As Mussolini's power increased, he began invading other nations. He believed that it was Italy's destiny to expand, just as it had during the Roman Empire.

Germany was also in economic disarray after World War I. By 1933, Adolf Hitler, called the *Fuehrer* (the "Leader," in German), had modeled his government after Mussolini's fascist government. Hitler created the Nazi Party and took power in Germany. He and his henchmen, called the Brownshirts, crushed everyone who did not agree with the Nazis, first inside the country and then outside.

Hitler began building his military and secret police, conquering as many nations as he could. While many countries opposed him, some countries, like Italy, joined him. Italy and Germany formed the Axis, an alliance between nations, in November of 1936, even before Italy joined Germany in war. The Axis nations would later include Japan. The Axis began aggressively invading and occupying nations in Europe and in the South Pacific. These antagonistic actions resulted in the retaliation of other nations, the Allies, which led to World War II.

Our story begins before Mussolini's declaration of war. Though war in Europe had begun long before, in my mother's remote village of Eglio, it was still a peaceful time, untouched by the turmoil in the rest of the world. But all things change. For the citizens of Eglio, change would come gradually once a new war began.

Chapter 1

Wonderful days like these in my beloved village in the hills of northern Tuscany are the ones that I remember and cherish the most. Good days, surrounded by my family. I smile to myself as I imagine opening the bedroom shutters to gaze out into the valley below as I had done hundreds of times before, my mother and brothers and sisters downstairs. A beautiful spring day, crisp and pristine. The rolling hills spread before me like folds in a giant carpet, punctuated with snow capped mountains in the distance. Miniature towns and villages dot the green landscape as if placed there by strokes of a brush on a painting. I take a deep breath and draw in the smell of the earth from which I came. The red soil of the tiered hillsides grows our food and nourishes us, our family, our citizens. The quiet majesty of Garfagnana is like an elixir. I am part of it and it is part of me. It always will be.

The days spent with my beloved family, in my treasured village in Tuscany before the start of the Second World War are the ones I value the most, because we were at our most innocent.

એર

Ding, dong, clang! Ding, dong, clang! The bells in the tower rang out their familiar peel, heralding the end of Easter Sunday services. The participants left our little church soon after, eagerly heading home to an indulgent holiday lunch. There were more people than usual because some had returned home to Eglio for the holiday from their work in the cities and abroad.

As my sister Mery and I emerged from the little grotto chapel into the brilliant early spring sunlight, I was as happy as any eleven-year-old could be because my entire family would be home — all six of my siblings. They would be there until the next day, an entire day of comfort and security, of sharing old stories, laughter and gossip, before they had to return to work at all their various places of employment outside the village. It made my *mamma* so happy to have us all at home together. It happened rarely because most of my brothers and sisters were all grown and quite independent. All of them worked; except for me and Mery. We were the youngest. Mery was four years older and, unlike me, one of the most beautiful girls in the village.

We removed our scarves once we were outside the church and let our hair flow freely in the warm spring breeze. Our friends waved to us. "Happy Easter! And to your families, too," they shouted before walking home. Our older sisters and Mamma had gone to the earlier mass that Easter Sunday, as they had a large meal to prepare for the rest of us for lunch, a daunting task. My brothers had attended the Easter Vigil mass last evening.

As we left the little church, Mery gave her friend Mario a shy last glance before clasping my arm and hurrying me forward. Intensely curious, I puzzled about it as we bustled home.

"Mery, I saw Mario pretending not to watch you during mass," I said innocently.

"Quiet, Bruna!" snapped Mery, furrowing her brow. "He was doing no such thing. Now hurry up and let's get home." But I saw the far side of Mery's full lips curl slightly into a smile as she looked away.

Our pace quickened on the sloping cobbled path as we moved closer to home, impatient for the festivities to begin. All that week, Mamma had been very busy cooking our favorite goodies. Before every sacred holiday, she and the other women in Eglio took turns using the cavernous local bakery ovens to cook their wild boar, torts, and breads. Our entire village was enveloped with a delicious aroma for days before the celebration.

As we rounded the corner at Evelina's house, Mery inhaled a long breath. "Mmh!" her nose pointed toward home. "Bruna, I can smell the rice and potato torts from here. Can you?" she asked, turning to me and smiling broadly.

I sniffed the air. "Yes. It's heavenly. I think Mamma is the best cook. I'm so hungry," I announced, dramatically, holding my stomach. On holidays such as this, I felt a keen richness in my soul. Though we were poor, Mamma worked hard to provide us with all the little extras at feast days. Even without a father to provide for us, we nonetheless felt we lacked nothing.

Mery and I chattered away as we hopped from one stone to another in our best shoes. The ruckus coming from our little house was hard to miss. Suddenly, Mery stopped. She grasped my arm and halted, fixing her gaze intently toward the house. "Is that — " Mery stopped in mid-sentence for effect. "Why, I thought I heard…"

I stared at my sister. "What?" I demanded. "Heard what?"

"Nora! I hear Eleonora," said Mery, wide-eyed. "She's arrived! She must have come while we were at mass. Now everyone's here!"

The two of us bolted for the double door. Mery was the first to get to it. She threw it open and burst inside. I was on her heels.

The sight that greeted us was glorious. There were our older brothers and sisters, some standing, some sitting on stools or stairs — wherever they could find space in the tiny kitchen — engaged in boisterous conversation. Aurelia was the eldest sister at twenty-seven, followed by Cesar, who was twenty-five. Eleonora was the next in line at twenty-three, then Pina, twenty-one. Alcide was born four years after Pina, which made him seventeen.

Mamma was bent over the hearth, tending lovingly to the simmering first course of the feast, a delicious beef stew, or *spezzatino*, complete with carrots, potatoes, and sweet onions.

She reveled in having her seven children all together.

"Here are the little ones! Look there!" came a shout from Aurelia as she tugged on Eleonora's arm.

"How lovely you two look in your best dresses," cooed Pina, peeking around one of my brother's shoulders. Pina had a smile that could light up the dreariest of rooms.

"Well, what did the old priest have to say this morning? More fire and brimstone? We're all going to hell?" Alcide was a tease. Mamma delivered a half-hearted smack to his arm. Cesar, strong and fearless, chortled at the sight of our slightly built mother cuffing his large, younger brother. Alcide, as tall as a lamppost, was the joker of the bunch, with a shock of black hair and a natural flair for narrating and embellishing the most ordinary of events. Cesar was shorter and stockier than Alcide, but strong. Cesar was the man of the house, since our father did not live with us. When my mother and the children returned to Eglio, our father had decided to stay in Brazil, where my siblings were all born.

"Silence now, Alcide!" Mamma said, with mild disapproval. She motioned to the two of us, still in the doorway. "Look how they've grown, Eleonora."

"They are even more beautiful than when I last was here," Nora smiled, her lovely cheekbones prominent with perpetual roses. She put out her cigarette and walked toward us, but we were already running to her. "Come and give me a hug. It seems like years since I've seen you." We all embraced tenderly in the crowded kitchen.

"I'm so happy you're home, Nora," said Mery, hugging her.

"I missed you, Nora," I said, holding onto her waist. I loved her the most. She was the loveliest and kindest to me and I could never get enough of her company. "Why can't you take care of the orphans around here? Then you could be closer to us." I looked up at her with puppy eyes, hoping I could convince her to live back home.

Eleonora was dedicated to her work as a nurse in a home for unwed mothers and abandoned children run by the Italian government. Unwed pregnant women were given support, no questions asked. After their babies were born they could decide whether to keep them or give them up for adoption.

"But the children need me in Florence, my treasure," she replied, gently cupping my face in her hands. "I can't just leave them."

"I suppose," I said, surrendering her to the poor little waifs I imagined in the orphanage. "But Armando misses you, too." Everyone burst into laughter. Armando had a crush on Eleonora, and she made it a point to see him whenever she came home from Florence. Armando was as handsome as Nora was beautiful. When they were together, it was as if one of those glamorous couples from the cinema had descended upon our ordinary little village.

Nora tucked a stray lock of dark hair that had escaped her coifed finger waves behind her ear. "You are all horrible busybodies," she said, smiling. "I shall ignore that. Now let's help Mamma with lunch. You two," she pointed to Cesar and Alcide, "can go outside. But don't go too far. We're eating soon." Nora was a natural leader.

"Mery and Bruna," called Mamma. "Go and change your clothes."

Mery and I climbed up the stairs to change into our day dresses and aprons. We were always careful not to create more work for Mamma. In addition to working in the fields, she took in washing for some of the women in the village for a little extra emergency money.

As we changed, our sisters bustled about the tiny kitchen, chattering all the while. I could hear them clearly from the second-floor bedroom.

Aurelia, the eldest of my siblings, had come home just the night before from her job as a cook for a wealthy family in Pisa. She lived there, coming home whenever she could. "Maria, at the grocers, told me that Cesar and Ersilia are courting," she said. It sounded like she was speaking loudly on purpose.

My brothers sat just outside the front door on the little terrace, lined with my mother's cherished daisies and geraniums. "And what about you and Dante next door?" Cesar replied, as he exhaled puffs of smoke from his cigarette. Aurelia shouted something back at him in Portuguese. My brothers and sisters were fluent in Portuguese, the native language of Brazil, where they were all born and raised. This shout from Aurelia gave rise to yet another peel of laughter from everyone except me. I was the only sibling born outside of Brazil, and I didn't understand a word.

"Speaking of Dante, do you remember last month?" Alcide snickered just recalling the incident. There was always another funny tale to tell. "After we left the bar? It was you, me,

Mario, and Dante." He was laughing so hard he could barely get the words out. Cesar was smiling. He knew the incident in question. The girls listened from the kitchen as they put the finishing touches on our feast.

"It was late and we had all had a few drinks. The village was quiet and we were headed home. We had stopped to talk outside of Egidio's door and Dante told a joke. We didn't realize how loud we were. I guess Egidio had had enough of telling us to be quiet. He came charging out in his underwear." Alcide guffawed, tears streaming down his face.

Cesar chimed in to finish the story. "He was absolutely furious. He glared at us in his baggy underwear," Cesar said mimicking poor Egidio, with an exaggerated grimace. "Then he pointed his finger at us. We thought he was going to call the police. Instead, jabbing his finger at each of us, he shouted, 'One, two, three, and four.' Then he just turned around, stormed back into his house, and slammed the door behind him. That was it! The four of us howled so loudly afterwards, we had to run home." Cesar was in tears retelling the story.

"What on earth did he mean by doing that?" asked Pina, laughing mostly at her brothers who were in stitches.

"Obviously, he wanted us to know that he would deal with each of us in the morning. It must have been cold out there in his long underwear," cackled Alcide, wiping the tears from his cheeks with a handkerchief.

"What about that time Guazzelli put a jacket on the sheep?" Alcide hollered, as he continued the anecdotes. There was hardly a need to recount that story, as everyone knew what Edo had done. The fun was in sharing it again.

But further stories had to wait.

"Come now, all to table. It's time to eat," I heard Eleonora announce from the kitchen below. The mad rush to secure a good spot at the Easter feast was on.

Chapter 2

Pina and Aurelia placed piping hot vessels of stew, and warm potato and rice tortes, fortified with lots and lots of *ricotta* and *parmigiano* cheese on the crowded table. Not to be left out, Eleonora offered crisp greens with sweet tomato salad, fresh baked bread and sharp, salty olives. Mamma grasped the carafe of wine from the shelf near the window and placed it on the table, alongside a jug of fresh water. The feast was ready.

After we said grace, the eight of us dove in. I was most interested in the cake that followed, a delicious *buccellato* pound cake made with fresh milk from our cow, eggs from our chickens, and lots of creamy butter.

After much initial clattering of cutlery against our plates, compliments to the cooks, and lip-smacking, the conversation predictably turned to a popular topic in our house whenever our family had the good fortune of coming together: politics.

"We are so busy these days in the steel factory," said Pina between mouthfuls of potato torte.

"Of course," responded Cesar. "If we go to war, there will be a demand for steel. Rifles, bullets, tanks."

"Oh, my goodness, Cesar. Don't say that." Mamma placed a finger over her lips. "I couldn't bear the thought of you two going off to war. I don't believe Il Duce is interested in going to war. Hitler is doing well on his own." This kind of talk made me very nervous.

"I wouldn't be so certain, Mamma," Alcide said, shaking his head. "There is talk in the factory about massive shipments…"

Nora interrupted him in mid-sentence with a kick under the table. Her eyes swept over to Mery and me. We had stopped eating, our eyes darting from one speaker at the table to the next.

"Mamma, is there going to be war here?" I wanted so badly to hear a no.

"Here? Up here in Eglio?" Mamma shook her head from side to side. Her tone made the idea of fighting in our little corner of the world seem silly. "Besides, Mussolini has always helped provide for us. We have all that we need. He cares for his people. We must trust him."

"Yes," said Eleonora softly. "He is the one who provides for the women and children at the orphanage where I work." I nodded, temporarily soothed, and concluded that Il Duce would not put my family, and in particular my brothers, in harm's way. "Well, enough of this talk. It's Easter, we must be happy. Let us *cin cin* to our health." Nora held up her glass. The rest of us hoisted our mismatched glasses in the air and toasted, *alla salute,* to our health.

"Speaking of health, did you hear what happened to the midwife in Sassi?" Pina asked, a smile creeping over her lips.

"Oh, now that's a story," Mery giggled.

"Tell us, Mery. What happened?" Aurelia was already beginning to snicker.

"Norina's bull, the one they use for breeding, got loose and terrorized the entire town. Everyone was indoors hiding from that wild animal," Mery said, trying not to laugh. "The poor midwife, having just assisted at a birth, knew nothing about it. She left the house and was cornered by the crazy bull in the archway between the piazza and the post office."

"Oh, the poor woman," gasped Mamma. "Did she get hurt?"

"No, but I hear they've asked her to run at the next Olympics," Cesar said, straight-faced. At this the entire kitchen was in stitches.

Mamma begged us all to lower our voices. Though she knew it was all in good fun, it was very important to her that her brood was always beyond reproach and that we behaved in an exemplary manner. Mother cared very much about what people thought of us. Perhaps it was because we were the only family in the village without a father. Or at least without a father who lived with us.

Chapter 3
A LITTLE BACKGROUND

My parents, Matilde and Aurelio, had emigrated to Sao Paolo, Brazil shortly after they married in 1912. An uncle had offered Aurelio employment in one of his businesses there. Aurelio, an only child from a relatively wealthy family, had decided to begin a new life in that far-away country with his new bride. He had been spoiled by his mother, Serafina, after his father died. As a young man, my father attended a boarding school in France, while his mother tended to the family business in partnership with her sisters. Successful businesswomen of that time, the sisters owned a number of small hotels, *pensioni,* in the Liguria resort region of Italy, in Florence, and in France.

When Aurelio had completed his education and it came time for him to join the family hotel business, he was expected to work his way up. An educated man, he didn't take kindly to that notion. Aurelio wouldn't agree to carry the guests' suitcases or walk the hotel dogs. Because of his refusal to do such menial work, a rift between the sisters developed. Eventually his mother gave up her share of the business. She and her new husband purchased a large property in the agrarian region of Garfagnana in Tuscany. They settled in the village of Eglio and worked the land.

My mother, Matilde, on the other hand was a simple, uneducated girl from the village. But she was beautiful and obedient. Unlike his mother, she was quiet and dutiful, qualities Aurelio valued most in women. Before long the couple fell in love and were married, though Aurelio's mother felt that he deserved better. Matilde had never learned to read or write, since she had always helped with the family farm rather than attending school.

Shortly after the newlyweds reached their new home in Brazil, Aurelio set to work at one of his uncle's brick factories as a supervisor and Matilde gave birth to their first child. Life was a struggle at first, but eventually their lives fell into place. The next year Matilde gave birth to another child. Before long another followed and then another. The years passed. Aurelio worked and came home to his family, where he was well looked after by his wife. He was an authoritarian figure to his wife and children and could be severe at times. Although Matilde took care of the household and tried not to complain, her health began to fail. The stifling heat of the unforgiving Brazilian climate and her ever-increasing brood were taking a toll. By then there were six children, two boys and four girls.

She longed to be back home, on the cool green hillside of her village, looking across at the sprawling valley before her. She missed the mountain air, fresh and aromatic with the scent of wildflowers and she longed for her sisters. She loved her husband and children, but her heart ached for the mountains as she steadily grew weaker.

Though her doctor warned Aurelio that she should not have any more children, Matilde soon learned that she was to have another child. She was now forty-one years of age, sick, and tired. She tried to overcome her malaise, but it was a losing battle. The physician came again and told Aurelio that if Matilde did not go back home to Italy, she would surely die. Delaying the trip was considered, but the physician insisted if she didn't make it home before the baby was born, she would die in childbirth. So, Aurelio took pity on his wife and made the necessary arrangements for her return to Italy. He decided that the children would go with her and he would follow once he had sold their belongings and his paper work was in order.

By the time Matilde boarded the ship back to Italy, her belly was enormous. She and the children said their tearful good-byes to Aurelio and excitedly boarded the ocean liner back to Italy. They had no idea that they would never see him again.

As the ship cut through the water, day after day, Matilde felt better and better. The salty sea air was therapeutic and she spent much time on deck with the children. The older ones always helped her, as by then some were in their teens. The closer the ship got to the cliffs of Gibraltar, the better she felt. One day, she began to feel the familiar pain in her back and belly. She knew that her baby was coming. The ship's physician and nurses were terribly excited, as this would be the second baby to be born on this voyage. It would be a first for the doctor *and* the ship's captain.

On April 14, 1929, on the Atlantic Ocean, on the magnificent ship, *Belvedere*, Bruna Maria Serafina Margherita Emilia Pucci was born. That was me! Mamma always liked the name Bruna. Maria, was after the captain's wife; Serafina, after Aurelio's mother; Margherita and Emilia, after the ship's nurses.

I loved hearing that story from my mother and I asked her to repeat it often. It made me feel very special, knowing that I was born in the middle of the ocean. None of my friends or siblings could claim that fact. It set me apart from everyone else.

I was the youngest child in a family of seven, raised by a single mother. This was a rarity in rural Tuscany at that time. I was as innocent and sheltered as any child in that pastoral setting could be. Life was good for me and my family, but the good days were numbered.

PART TWO

Italy Enters the War
1940 – 1942

When Nazi Germany invaded Poland in September 1939, Great Britain and France declared war on Germany. Throughout 1940, Nazi troops continued to systematically seize other nations and take control. Countries, such as Denmark, Norway, Holland, and Belgium, were no match for the German forces. They all surrendered, toppling over like dominoes. In the meantime, Nazi bombing campaigns began on the British Isles, while their troops prepared to invade France. Italy's Benito Mussolini held out from joining the war until the last moment. Then, when he saw fascist victory on the horizon, he made up his mind and decided to join Hitler's war.

Four days after Mussolini's declaration of war on June 10, 1940, Nazi troops marched into Paris and shortly afterward

France surrendered. In September 1940, the German Air Force began all night air raid bombing campaigns in London. Meanwhile, Italy invaded Greece in addition to other countries in North Africa. In 1941 the Axis powers invaded Soviet territory, creating another front. All the while, Nazi forces continued their relentless persecution of Jews.

That same year, the United States declared war on Japan after Japanese forces bombed Pearl Harbor in Hawaii — a surprise attack. The German/Italian/Japanese Axis appeared unstoppable. By 1942, the horrific conflict was the largest land war in history. Virtually the entire world was at war. The people of Eglio would now begin to feel the war as well.

Chapter 4

June 10, 1940, that horrible, detestable, wicked day; the day that began the washing away of our innocence, the tearing apart of my traditional adolescence; the day that would test my family's bonds to the limit. It had begun so unremarkably, so perfectly and ordinarily, that when I think back to our unspoiled simplicity, it makes me shudder. It was over with the speed of a radio signal cutting through the valley. Before long, my sheltered life in a tiny Tuscan village would slip away as subtly as the morning fog crept over the Apennine Mountains.

ஒ

When I reached the cobble path that led to my house, I paused and steadied my breathing. My hand shielded my eyes from the early morning sun, still low on the horizon. I scanned the steep, meandering descent to *Poggetti,* the name we gave our home. The name was derived from the verb, *poggiare*, which means to lean or perch upon. The little house we lived in was literally perched on the lower portion of Eglio, on the edge of an ancient retaining wall facing the expansive valley below. Ours was a very close community. Eglio's population that year, 1940, had come very close to surpassing 500, including those living in the outlying farming areas as well.

I skipped merrily along the path, holding fast to the freshly ground sack of chestnut flour in my arms. Mamma had sent me to the mill to have some dried chestnuts ground into flour. If there was one thing in abundance in the forest around Eglio, it was chestnut trees, and the villagers took full advantage of anything growing wild that could supplement their food supply.

I did a lot of thinking as I walked. I thought of my sisters and brothers and my mamma. I thought about how my father had decided to stay to work in Brazil, since there was no work for him in Italy. Occasionally he sent us money, and I would look forward to his letters, which he would send both to me and my siblings. Since I never lived with my father, I didn't really miss him, though I *did* miss never having met him.

These thoughts preoccupied me, as I walked from the miller. I knew that Mamma had probably sent me to the mill just to give me something to do. It was boring for me with only one sister in the house. Mery was getting older and she didn't want much to do with me, her baby sister, anymore. She and Eleonora had always been most popular at the impromptu dances. These dances were held in the theater, where sometimes a few of the men in the village would sit with an accordion or two and start playing. The place really was a theater, used by the villagers in both Eglio and neighboring Sassi for plays and skits. We occasionally enjoyed a drama or a comedy by a core group of amateur actors, who mounted plays like *La signora delle Camelie*, "The Lady of the Camellias," for all of us to enjoy. It was an old cavernous space, its exposed wooden beams and whitewashed walls lovingly maintained by the villagers. It was the only building big enough in the town to accommodate a large group of people.

I especially looked forward to the dance celebrations after feast days, like the one coming up in August. It was the Feast of Santa Maria, our town patron saint. On this day, there was high mass in the church, followed by a procession with the statue of Mary through the town. Rice and potato tortes were served and then the dance began. Nearly everyone in the village would attend, married or single. It was a time to take a break from the everyday routine and share a dance with one's spouse or sweetheart. Heavenly! But I was still young and most of the time, I only watched everyone else, like the other young girls and boys my age had to. I reckoned that no matter how old I was, I would always be the baby of the family.

"Good morning, Evelina." My tone was cheerful as I walked by my neighbor's open door. My pace slowed when

I noticed that she had a bulky bunch of clothes in her arms.

"Hello, Bruna," the old woman smiled as she struggled to keep the soap bar and washboard balanced on top of the heap of clothes.

I set the flour down on the side of the cobble path. "Let me help you with that. I'll carry the soap and washboard to the laundry tub for you," I said, eagerly grabbing the washboard from the top of the laundry pile. As I watched in horror, the washboard caught on the knotted sheet with which Evelina had secured the bundle. The entire basket and contents toppled to the ground. Shirts, housedresses, socks and underwear scattered everywhere.

"I'm so sorry, Evelina," I gasped, mortified. Straight away I lunged forward to gather up the clothes. Before I could even begin, the old woman's hand reached down and gently tapped me on the shoulder.

Evelina sighed. "If you don't mind, Bruna, I can bring it all to the tub myself. Thank you though, for the offer," she added patiently, shaking her head slowly from side to side. She bent down to reassemble her wash bundle.

"Of course — if you insist. I'm so sorry again. Good morning." I scooped up the sack of flour and swiftly resumed my way home without looking back. That entire awkward display was typical for me.

Why do I constantly make a pest of myself? I questioned. My cheeks turned red. Why was I so clumsy and gawky? I was just eleven, but some of the girls my age in the village had already begun to mature. My sister Mery was fifteen, but she looked twenty. She was beautiful, like one of those movie actresses from Hollywood in America. Everyone said how beautiful Mery was. But, I was just Bruna, the ugly, skinny, tanned baby of the family.

Shoulders slumped, I tramped down the last set of steps and turned the corner on the path to my left, past Oreste and Ida's house built into the same rock as ours. I inhaled the wonderful aroma of fresh bread baking in the little hearth oven. Mamma made her own bread, and sometimes she made *polenta*, a porridge made from corn meal. But today, for me, it would be chestnut meal.

I walked slowly, distracted by my thoughts, under the kitchen window and past my mother's abundant geraniums that adorned the *terrazza*, overlooking the dirt road below. Looking over the wrought-iron barrier down to the road, I thought of my brothers negotiating the steep hill on their bicycles in the early morning, while it was still dark. I loved them because they protected me, and our mother.

"Mamma, I'm home," I called out. The little kitchen consisted of a simple basin and a wood stove. An oversized table and a variety of chairs and stools stood pushed against the back wall. It wasn't necessary to pull the table away from the wall unless all my siblings were there at one time, an increasingly rare happening.

Aurelia had found work as a cook for a wealthy family in Pisa and came home when she could. And Pina worked in the steel factory at Fornaci di Barga. The town's name literally meant the furnaces of Barga. The steel factories had

33

become very busy with the possibility of war breaking out at any moment. Pina stayed in a rooming house with four of her friends from the village and would come home on Fridays after her last shift.

My brothers Cesar and Alcide worked at the factory in Fornaci di Barga, too. But they made the daunting ride on their bicycles back up to Eglio every evening after work. Cesar would come back every night, because he felt a keen obligation to Mamma and to us younger siblings. Alcide was just too young to venture out on his own. Even though he was very tall and imposing, barely able to get through the doorway, Mamma would sometimes jokingly say that he was afraid of his own shadow.

As I set the chestnut flour down on the scrubbed table, I wondered if Evelina would tell mother about the laundry. That nagging worry about what the rest of the village thought of me usually served to preoccupy me at least once or twice a day.

"I'm coming, Bruna," Mamma answered, as she gingerly descended the stairs. Her arthritis had been bad lately, and she had to be cautious when she used the stairs. The flights of steps to the second and third floors were extremely steep, almost like a ladder. The house itself was built against the hillside and one of its walls was the rock face of the mountain. It was a sturdy house built with mortar and brick and stones from the hillside. It was whitewashed inside and the roof was made of red clay tile. Its shutters on the neat little windows were green, like the fields in the valley.

This was my mother's family home. Though it had three floors, it was small but served our purpose. The first floor consisted of the kitchen and my sisters' bedroom with a single and a double bed. The second floor had one bedroom for my mother and me, and the third floor was the boys' bedroom. We had no indoor plumbing and brought water from the fountain in the *piazza* for cooking and bathing. Our outhouse was located farther down the pathway, out of sight. It was a very modest home, but we all made do and were content.

"Heaven help us, Bruna, but these stairs are getting steeper every day," proclaimed Mamma, sighing and grasping the simple wooden banister.

"No, Mamma, they just feel that way to you. Here," I said climbing the first few steps to reach up and assist her. "Hold my hand." She readily accepted my help.

"You know, Mamma, I think I'll go to *Nonna* and *Nonno's* tonight. Nonna made cheese yesterday. Perhaps she will make *foccaccia* bread to go with it." I loved goat cheese and foccaccia almost as much as I loved my grandmother and especially my grandfather.

"As you wish, dear. Just don't get in their way," she warned.

My mother dressed in a simple manner. She wore her skirts close to her ankles and when she was home she always wore an apron. Her long hair was braided and worn in a tight bun at the base of her skull. Sometimes I looked at her and thought that she looked much older than her years.

"Let's get started," she said smiling at me as she opened up the bag. She peered into the sack. "Looks like the miller did a fine job," she said. "The chestnut porridge will be good this time."

Mamma busied herself with measuring out the portions of flour and other ingredients for lunch, while I got the kindling ready in the fireplace. It would need to burn a while so that the embers were hot enough to cook the meal over the grills. Mamma would work the simple mixture of chestnut meal, goat's milk, butter, and sugar in a bowl as I sat on one of the mismatched chairs watching her, my head resting on folded hands on the tabletop.

"When will it be ready, Mamma?" I asked. "I'm hungry."

"Soon," she answered patiently and glanced at me with kindly eyes. "Meanwhile, why don't you go and check your collars. You will need to wash them before school tomorrow."

"Yes, Mamma," I answered obediently. I did not need to spend much more time washing my collars nightly. It was June, and soon school would be over for the summer. This made me both excited and sad. I enjoyed it when my siblings came home for summer holidays, but I also loved school and would miss it. As I turned to walk up the stairs, it struck me that I could make an event of the trip to wash my collars and see what my friends were up to.

Chapter 5

I scurried up the stairs to the second floor and walked sideways around the bed to the little bureau I shared with my mother. Beside it was a basket of clothes to be washed. I gently pulled out the familiar collars that were part of my school uniform. The girls all had to wear white collars and black tunics. The boys wore black shirts and ties. This is how the *piccole italiane* or Italian youth were required to dress. It was very important to Il Duce that we wore black. It was the color of his party, the fascists.

Everyone said that Il Duce was a great man because he had improved job opportunities and the economy for the common people. But there were also rumblings about his association with the German Fuehrer, Adolf Hitler. People said that

Mussolini would support Hitler even if it meant war for Italy. This frightened me. If there was a war, my brothers would be called to defend the country.

"I have the collars, Mamma." I dashed back down the stairs.

"Good," she said as she prepared the meal in the cast iron pan. "Your lunch will be cooked and ready when you come back."

I stooped under the kitchen basins and found a bar of homemade lye soap. I put it in a small hamper with the collars and some of my personal things to be washed. "Be back soon."

The public *lavatoio,* or washtub fountain, was a very large oval basin, about the size of ten large wash tubs, located centrally in the village. It had continuously running cold water flowing from a pipe, replenishing the huge basin with fresh water. The women would arrive very early in the morning to get the cleanest water for washing their family's clothes. There was a ledge around the entire basin so that clothes could be soaped up, scrubbed, pounded, and rinsed one by one.

By now the sun was high in the sky, sending its rays down on the whitewashed village. On my way to the wash tub, I decided to collect my best friends, Armida and Beppina. Nobody said that I couldn't enjoy myself while working. With basket in hand, I found the familiar shortcuts through the steep inclines winding around Eglio's houses, many built right into the hillside, just like ours.

I skipped lightly up the steps in my wooden clogs to Armida's house first. *Clip, clop, clip clop!* They could hear me coming. Armida stuck her head out one of the upper windows as she heard my familiar gait. "Hey," Armida smiled and waved down at me. "Are you coming my way?"

I motioned with a nod to the bundle in my hands. "I am! Do you have wash, too?"

"Wait there. I'll be right down." She closed the shutters slightly, and then disappeared inside. While I headed to the front door to wait for her, I heard another familiar voice.

"Hello down there." It was Armida's big sister, Eva. She was the most beautiful girl in the village, even more stunning than Mery, and her smile could light up the sun. She was fifteen years of age and all the boys in the village would forget their own names when she walked by.

"Hello, Eva," I nodded up to her. "Will you be in sewing tomorrow?"

"Of course," Eva said as she shot a fleeting glance in the direction of Beppina's house further up the path. Everyone knew that she and Beppina's brother secretly liked each other, but neither would dare to admit it. "I must get to work on my linens for my hope chest." All the girls in the village learned to embroider their sheets, pillowcases and tablecloths for their future marriages.

I furrowed my brow. "I can't wait to be able to embroider. The seamstress is still having me do hems for her." I looked up at Eva with a grimace.

Eva laughed heartily. "Don't worry little one. Your time will come." Sometimes, I wished that my own sister Mery would speak to me so kindly. But, I supposed, sisters were not ordinarily that kind to one another openly, though they still loved each other dearly as I knew Mery loved me.

Armida stepped out the door. "Come on," she said, as she slipped her arm through mine, balancing her basket of clothes. "Let's go get Beppina."

Armida, Beppina, and I were inseparable friends and we did just about everything together. We lived innocently in the shadow of our church tower. We washed our clothes, chatting more than washing. We talked of our parents, our siblings, teachers, and the boys in whom we were interested. We sometimes spoke secretly of our menstrual cycles, but never in the open.

"I wish that Ugo and Eva would have the courage to admit that they like each other," Beppina sighed as she rinsed out her last apron. Then suddenly she gasped, turned to Armida and grabbed her hand. "What if they get married!" she said dreamily, staring into the distance. "Then we'd be sisters."

"That's true!" exclaimed Armida. "Wouldn't that be wonderful," she squealed. She held Beppina's hand to her heart.

"I want to be your sister, too!" I cried.

"You have too many sisters already," laughed Beppina. We broke out in laughter, but soon Beppina took on a graver tone. She glanced surreptitiously over her shoulder. Then she leaned in to us and said, almost in a whisper, "I need to tell you something that I overheard my brothers talking about last night." She checked over her shoulder once more to make certain that no one was listening. "I heard him say that Il Duce is very close to entering the war. And any day now, Italy will be at war, just like Germany."

I gasped. "Oh, no. Don't say such things. That would be wretched." I shook my head in disbelief. I shuddered. "What would happen to our brothers? They would have to fight, wouldn't they?"

"I'm sure they would," said Armida. "But Il Duce and the Fuehrer know what is best. They love their people and we must trust them." She spoke the words, but her voice gave away her uncertainty.

We had been told to trust and love Mussolini, but I could not support my brothers being put in harm's way for any reason. "Let's not talk about it anymore," I said, getting a queasy feeling in my stomach. "After all, it might not happen." I wanted to go home now, to my mother and to the security of Poggetti. Everything always seemed safe there. I began to gather my things, placing the pristinely washed white collars in the basket to bring home to hang dry. "I must get home for lunch. Mamma is preparing chestnut meal for me." There was now a gray cloud hanging over my mood. I detested talk of the imminent war. It frightened me.

"And I must hurry home," answered Armida, with a shrug. "Schoolwork."

"Me too," said Beppina. "See you in school tomorrow, then."

"If you can, come to the library at Alfezio's this afternoon." I kissed my friends on the cheek and turned to go home. But as I walked, I couldn't rid my mind of the thought of war. My pace quickened as my thoughts raced. As I got closer to my little house on the edge of the village, I was running and breathless.

"Mamma!" I shouted as I tore inside. "Mamma!" I set the basket on the floor haphazardly and scurried from the stairs to the bedrooms and back down to find her. "Mamma!" I shouted again as she rushed into the kitchen from outside, startled by the urgency in my voice.

"What is it, Bruna?" she asked, worried.

"Oh, Mamma!" I cried as I rushed to her and flung my arms around her.

"What's wrong?" She was almost knocked off balance by my lunge.

"Mamma! Something terrible is going to happen. Beppina told Armida and me that her brother said that Il Duce will go to war. If this is true, then Cesar and Alcide will have to become soldiers, won't they?" The tears were streaming now.

Mamma shook her head. She hugged me tightly and attempted a smile. "There, there now." She stroked my back soothingly. "Don't worry about such things." She held me at arm's length so that she could see my eyes. She smiled down at me and kissed my forehead. Her eyes were so wise and kind.

"You are too young to worry about such things. No more tears, little girl. Look, your lunch is waiting and getting cold." Mamma motioned to the plate of meal on the table, a spoon beside it with the sugar bowl nearby. "Promise me you won't think about it any longer. It won't do any good to worry anyway." She gently nudged me.

I wiped my tears on my sleeve and walked half-heartedly to the steaming bowl. I couldn't be farther from hungry if I tried, but I ate anyway. Food should not be wasted.

Mamma sat beside me and tried as best as she could to distract me from the troubling gossip. I knew that she was worried too, but she dared never let it show. Mother always protected me. "Now that you've eaten, don't you feel better?" she asked.

"Yes," I answered, wiping my mouth and drinking the last of my goat's milk. "I think I'll go to Alfezio's library after I hang up the wash. Maybe if I find a book to read, it will take my mind off of all this."

"That is an excellent idea. Find a good book to read. It will fill up your head and push all the bad things out through your ears." We both laughed at the notion. "Perhaps you can read to me and Ida tonight." Ida was our neighbor next door. She spent many an evening with us in our warm little house. Sometimes she bustled to her house next door and fixed a plateful of chestnut meal with a dash of hot goat's milk and a pinch of sugar, as a treat. Like my mother, she couldn't read either.

Chapter 6

Alfezio was a well-educated man. He had served in the army in the Great War of 1915-1918 and had survived a bombing. Although he escaped with his life, his leg was badly injured and the doctors had to amputate it. The government had given him an artificial wooden one. In his lifetime, Alfezio had collected many books and had amassed quite an extensive assortment. He didn't mind sharing them with others. Eventually the villagers called the first floor of his family home "the library."

Once my clean things were hung outside in the warm sun to dry, I removed my apron and ambled up the path to the village center. *Clip, clop, clip, clop* in my wooden shoes. As I walked past the houses, I could hear snippets of conversations.

"…it may not be practical to go to the butcher until tomorrow…"

"…what would your father say if he knew you had…"

"…this Sunday I think I will wear this to…"

Conversations of an ordinary day. People living, day-to-day, not knowing what was to come in the future. I walked at an easy pace and glanced up at Evelina's house. *Her* laundry was not hung out to dry. She must not have gotten to the washtub after all.

I turned the familiar corner to my left and walked along the main road of the village, ever on an incline going uphill. As I got closer to the general store, I could hear the radio crackling and blaring. There was the ever-present sound of men's voices coming from Ferrari's bar, discussing politics and global issues as if they all had the answer to the world's problems. I stuck my head in to say "hello," and as always, everyone said "hello" back. Ferraro Ferrari and his wife, the proprietors, were busy serving their customers. It was the village meeting place. There was a familiar tune coming from the radio, a love song.

Alfezio's house was almost directly across the street from the bar. I knocked and opened the door without waiting for an answer. In our village, the doors were never locked and everyone was welcome inside at any time. "Permission to enter," I called. This was a courtesy, a warning of sorts that someone was about to enter the home.

"Come in," said a voice from behind a stack of books. Alfezio was at his desk, the afternoon sun streaming in from the crystal clean window behind him.

"Good afternoon, Alfezio," I announced. "I've come to borrow a book, if I may." I wondered how he could concentrate on what he was reading with the radio blaring from across the street.

"Help yourself, Bruna," he said, not looking up from his book. He looked extremely engrossed in what he was reading.

I began to look about at the shelves full of interesting titles. Some were old, some were new. All were intriguing to me, but today I was preoccupied. Knowing that Alfezio had been in the last war, I was curious about what it was like, but I hesitated to ask since that might be rude. I didn't know how he would react to my questions. After all, he had lost a leg and that was quite serious. Still, my inquisitiveness got the better of me. I circled around the room to where he was sitting. I pretended to be interested in the Renaissance poetry section.

"How are you today?" I asked, scanning the stacks. There were books by Dante and Petrarch. On the next shelf were science books.

"I am well. And yourself?" he replied. He allowed himself a slight glance in my direction. I noticed his cane placed strategically against the side of his desk.

"Well, thank you." I craned my neck to get a better look at his book. "What are you reading?"

"It is an old book. *The Odyssey* by Homer," he said patiently, looking up.

"Who was Homer?" I asked.

Alfezio chuckled. "He was a Greek philosopher who lived many years ago. He also wrote *The Iliad*."

46

"Well, he can't be that good. I've never heard of him."

Alfezio laughed out loud and closed his book. I couldn't understand what was so funny. He clasped his hands and folded them under his chin. "You are rarely this talkative, Bruna. Is there something on your mind?"

With a blush, I looked away. "I was just wondering…." As I started to speak, I turned my gaze toward a colorful picture dictionary, and pulled it halfway out of its spot, pretending I was interested in it. "You were in the Great War, weren't you?" I put the book back and pulled out another, still not looking at him. How odd was that question. Everyone knew that he had been in it. He had a wooden leg to prove it.

"Yes?" As if he knew that there was another question coming.

"And your leg, did it hurt…when it happened?" I gathered up the courage to look at him now. He looked thoughtful, his hands folded against his mouth.

"Very much," he answered. "But eventually the hurt went away." He tilted his head. "Why do you ask?"

"Just so that I understand," I shrugged. "In case it happens to someone I know." I looked away again, because I didn't want him to see the tears in my eyes.

"What do you mean?" he asked.

"So that I know what to expect for my brothers if they go to war…"

"Stop there, child." Alfezio cut me off in mid-sentence. "There is no sense worrying about something that may not happen." He took a deep breath and let it out in a sigh. "I've heard the rumors, too. The Blackshirts like to spread them to get everyone talking, but you should not worry before anything happens." He reached for his cane with one hand and grasped the side of his desk with the other. Carefully he pulled himself up and walked around to the front of his bureau so that he was facing me. He patted me on the head and smiled a kindly smile. "Find a book and read. It will take your mind off things. Look," he said, as he motioned to a shelf behind me, pointing out a colorful title. "Isn't that one of your favorites?"

I nodded and smiled back up at him. His mustache was curled at the ends. "Yes, it is." I turned around to wipe the tear away. "I will try to keep my mind off bad things," I sniffed. "Thank you for comforting me."

I chose a book by Carlo Collodi called *Pinocchio*. My mother loved that book. She would be pleased to hear it tonight. Feeling better now, I thanked Alfezio once more. It was understood that I meant for the conversation as well as the book. "You know, Alfezio, Pinocchio is one of my favorite characters and…" I stopped talking as I noticed that Alfezio had put a finger to his lips.

"Shh," he hissed as he listened and tilted his head towards the window. The music from the radio had stopped and there was a loud crackly voice blaring instead. All the other voices in the bar had stopped chattering. It sounded like there was an announcement on the wireless. A loud, authoritarian voice was speaking. It was Il Duce. I listened now, too.

"…The hour of destiny is striking in the skies above Italy. The hour of irrevocable decisions. The declaration of war has already been delivered to the ambassadors of Britain and France. We are going to war against the plutocratic and reactionary democracies of the West who have invariably hindered the progress and often threatened the very existence of the Italian people."

That was all I heard. I looked at Alfezio. His color had gone from a healthy blush to ashen gray in seconds. He looked at me, but did not speak. He only shook his head.

I held the book tight in my arms, as I heard cheers coming from the bar drowning out Mussolini's voice. My first childish thought was that obviously some of the men were happy at the prospect of losing a leg in another war.

Alfezio was speaking to me now, but my ears were buzzing. I couldn't hear him. He leaned on his cane so that his face was close to mine. He spoke again, but his words were in vain. All I could think of was getting home fast. I turned slowly and exited the library.

All of my nightmares had materialized in a matter of seconds. One minute I was happy to be reading *Pinocchio* to my mother that evening and the next there was the impending doom of war. My family might be torn apart. My breathing was shallow and I could feel the sweat on my brow. My stomach was churning queasily. Suddenly, I felt totally alone in my despair. I had to get back to Mamma. Mamma would know what to do. I would ask Mamma.

As I stood on the narrow street between the library and the bar, I noticed in my dazed stupor that people in the town were beginning to spill into the street. Metal latches clanked furiously, doors opened wide and women wailed and cried their despair, running to one another, gesticulating wildly, questioning the radio transmission as to whether it was really true. Had they heard right? Were their sons and husbands being sent to join the war?

Chapter 7

Soon after Il Duce's announcement, the draft notices calling the men in the village to serve their country began to arrive. Now all men between eighteen and fifty-four had to fight.

Mamma walked gingerly to the post box every day, hoping to put off the inevitable, but it was inescapable. Alcide was still too young, but twenty-five-year-old Cesar soon received his letter. It was late June and the bright sun coupled with the approaching warmth of summer made the gloomy event surreal in the dazzling light.

"God in heaven!" I heard Mamma exclaim one afternoon. She was at the door and I was upstairs in the bedroom changing after a day in my nonna's little plot of farmland. This was not typical for Mamma as she was usually very even tempered. I angled my head to peer downstairs.

"What is it, Mamma?"

"Heaven help us." I heard her voice tremble.

"Mamma? What?" No sooner had the words left my mouth than I guessed what it was. It was Cesar's letter. I heard Mamma crying.

I rushed downstairs to comfort her, putting my arm around her as she sat on the stoop half in and half out of the house. "Please Mamma, don't cry."

I could tell that she was trying very hard not to upset me, but I could see by her eyes that she too was extremely worried. "Oh, goodness." She wiped her tears with her apron. "I don't know why I'm carrying on like this. It's no surprise that this would come sooner or later."

"That's all right." It was my turn to comfort her. "Cesar is strong and brave. No one can hurt him." Deep in my heart, I believed every word and I knew I was right.

Later that afternoon, I was told to visit my grandparents, before the boys came home from work. Mamma tried hard to keep me from seeing she was upset, but I knew better. Still, if it gave her peace of mind to think that she spared me the heartache of seeing her cry when she gave my eldest brother the letter, I was willing to oblige. I could give her at least that much.

Separations like these soon became commonplace in Eglio. The letters arrived, the mothers cried, the fathers secretly fretted about losing their sons, but were proud to have them fight against the "enemy." We were told by Mussolini's Ministry of Popular Culture that we had an enemy and that the youth should learn to "believe, obey, fight." Mussolini is always right. I had heard this all my life. I had seen images of Mussolini as a good family man, photographed with his wife and children, as a musician playing the violin, as the hero of the peasants harvesting grain, and as the brave commander-in-chief flying a fighter plane.

Cesar soon left for his basic training. The base was near enough that he would be able to visit once in a while on leave. He was very brave and did not make a fuss when he left. Mamma cried for days afterwards, but I tried my best to be strong. After all Alcide was still home and now he would become the man of the house until he turned eighteen.

Italy had invaded southern France earlier that year. Cesar was soon stationed on the Italy/France border in the Alps as a guard in the Alpini troops, which were light infantry troops, specializing in mountain combat. He was fortunate because he was not directly in harm's way and because he was close to home. The army gave its soldiers many things: their uniforms, boots, rifles, backpacks filled with necessary gear. But best of all were the chocolate bars.

Rationing of food and resources had started soon after the war broke, so luxury items were in short supply. I eagerly awaited Cesar's visits not only to see him, but also for the rare treat of his chocolate bars. They were supposed to be a quick source of energy for the soldiers to keep them warm in the winter months. Never having much of a sweet tooth, Cesar would save his chocolates and bring them when he visited. And he gave them to me. I would save them and hide them in a shiny tin box that my grandmother had given me, carefully storing them away for a special occasion.

By Christmas time, I had filled the box with the tasty treats. This fact was not lost on Alcide.

"Hey, Bruna," he would say. "Come on, let's count your chocolate bars to see how many you have now." I was always delighted with the attention, since Alcide rarely gave me the time of day unless it was for a joke of some kind. I would run up to my room and carefully carry down the box. Since it was the Christmas season, we would sit by our modest little tree, adorned with oranges, nuts, bits of ribbon, and small home-made gifts, the fire burning cheerfully in our kitchen hearth, and start counting.

"Here, you count this pile and I will count these," he would say very seriously.

"All right. One, two, three, four…sixteen in total." My eyes gleamed. "You should have seventeen, because I counted thirty-three last time."

Alcide would press his lips together and shake his head pensively. "No, Bruna, I only have fifteen. You must have mis-counted. Try again." Though I counted again, my chocolate calculations never did balance. I couldn't understand this. I was sure my counts were accurate.

"Hey! You aren't taking them are you, Alcide?" I would ask with narrowed eyes. "While you're counting?"

"Me? No, I'm trying to help you!" he assured me. "But, I'll tell you a secret. I hear that mice love chocolate. I bet it's mice that are eating your chocolate." This would upset me immensely since I worked so hard to save the sweet treats, yet somehow they were slowly disappearing.

One day, Mamma overheard the exchange between my brother and me. My chocolate had dwindled down to five or six bars. I burst out crying. Mamma knew right away who the culprit was.

"Alcide, you horrid creature." She plucked up one of her tea towels and smacked him on the back of the head with it.

"Hey! What was that for?" He held the back of his head, feigning great injury.

"This is your mouse, Bruna. A very tall mouse named Alcide." I wailed for what seemed like forever when I discovered who was taking my chocolate bars. Needless to say, I never allowed Alcide near my chocolate box again.

∽

As the cold mountain winter gave way to spring, Eglio was still relatively untouched by the war raging in other parts of Europe. Our lives went on as usual, except for the missing men who had been sent off to fight for the cause. When Alcide turned eighteen, his conscription letter came too. Mamma was very concerned about Alcide. Some of the men were being sent far away and it was more difficult for them to get home for visits.

He did his military training and then word came that he would be stationed with the Italian forces on the island of Rhodes in the Aegean Sea near the Greek mainland. Il Duce's army had invaded Greece since the declaration of war. I feared for Alcide more than I had for Cesar. Aside from the fact that he was so much younger than Cesar, he just seemed more vulnerable. I could sense that my mother felt the same way.

The day came when he had to ship off. "Oh, my heavens," Mamma fretted, as we said our good-byes. "Why do you have to be so far away? Why all the way to Rhodes?" She wiped at her eyes as she let go of him.

"Just stay as far away from the enemy as you can," I said simply, as I stood beside Zelinda, Alcide's sweetheart.

"Well said, Bruna," she smiled down at me, then looked up at my towering brother. "You had better do as she says. And come back safe." They hugged each other before he turned to step in the truck that would take him back to his base.

"I will," was all he could manage to get out. His eyes were misting up. Alcide tried to be brave, but I could tell he was anxious. He tried to smile at us, a timid smile, as we parted. As the truck drove off, my brother's image blurred through my rising tears.

Chapter 8

Slowly things began to change. Some people were no longer as keen about the war as they had been at first. There were still the staunch fascists in our town who supported Il Duce without question. Husbands and sons, fathers and brothers left our village, leaving only the very young or old men, along with the women and children. This affected the village and its farmlands. Much of Eglio still relied on farming, and the farming still had to be done. The soil needed tilling and the crops needed to be planted and harvested, especially with food becoming more scarce all the time.

Our family was grateful that our grandparents had a plot of land on which they cultivated wheat, a variety of vegetables, and fruit trees, but not all of the families in Eglio were so fortunate.

Mamma had always worked in the fields, sometimes helping my grandparents on their land, or working for wealthy landowners. In this way she was able to save as much food for the winter as possible. Now her work in the fields became a necessity.

Once as I was walking to school in the autumn, Palmira, a landowner who lived in the upper part of the village, was heading to work in her family fields to harvest for the winter. Two of her sons had been drafted and she felt the heavy hand of war directly. She, her husband and their young daughter were left to reap their harvest of grain on their own.

"I need my sons back. I don't care what people say. Mussolini doesn't know what he's doing." She gave her negative opinion of Il Duce quite openly, which could be very foolish. I continued to walk to school in my black tunic and white collar uniform, hearing Palmira as she strode swiftly in the direction to her fields, muttering her curses.

"Palmira, you'd better keep that talk to yourself," snapped one of the villagers, still loyal to Il Duce.

"I will do no such thing!" she answered, defiant as ever. As time passed, many had come to feel the same way she did, but were hesitant to speak up for fear of reprisals from the Blackshirts.

As I walked, I noticed Edo Guazzelli striding down the steps from the center of town. Edo's family had lived in the village for generations. He was the second of five siblings; the eldest, Mario, had been drafted shortly before Alcide. Mario had helped to look after the family, as did many other first-born sons in the village. Now it was Edo who helped take care of the family, more every day since his mother was a sickly woman and his father had become ill. "Hello, Edo," I said in a guarded voice. I was still thinking about the exchange between Palmira and the villager.

"Hi, Bruna," he said, barely looking at me. "Off to school?"

"Yes. It's my last year." I was twelve years old and the fifth grade was the last year of school for many of us in the mountains. "Have you heard from Mario?" I had to pick up my pace to keep up with him as he moved toward the main road.

"No, not lately." Edo shook his head. "Father is worried. Mario has been sent far away to Russia, you know."

"Yes, I heard." His brother was such a good soul. "I'm sure he's all right." What else could I say?

"I hope so."

"Where are you off to?" I asked. He stopped for an instant to answer.

"To the forest, to cut some wood. I'm taking it to Castelnuovo to sell." Castelnuovo was a fairly large town to the north of us, downhill all the way. "I may be able to buy some oil for the family on the black market. There's no oil to be found around here."

I had heard of this "black market." Since everything was being rationed, scarce goods were being traded or bought illegally for a high price. My eyes widened with concern at this prospect.

"You must be careful, Edo. I hear that you can be punished if you're caught dealing in the black market."

Edo smiled. "The money from selling the wood is not only for that. I would like to study one day. I want to be a tool and die maker after the war."

"Good luck with that. You know, Cesar cut and sold wood in Castelnuovo, too," I told him. "That was before he worked at the factories in Fornaci di Barga. He told me that he would chop wood, walk all the way down to Castelnuovo to sell the wood. Then he would buy bread with the money and eat it on the way home."

Edo smiled and nodded. Then he waved at me and said, "Enjoy your last year at school." I nodded back shyly as he continued to walk to the main dirt road toward the woods and I continued on my way to the schoolhouse.

At seven in the morning sharp, the doors opened and our two teachers led an assortment of children from both Eglio and Sassi into the small building. Our day started with our pledge to Mussolini and our "fatherland." In addition to arithmetic and grammar, we were instructed in patriotism and the need for courageous action and had to study Il Duce's "Doctrine of Fascism." It was a philosophy that glorified war and rejected peace. We also had to study Mussolini's "Decalogue" which was modeled after the Ten Commandments.

It consisted of ten rules that stated the role and proper conduct of citizens. Citizens must obey, serve, and protect the government; citizens must protect Il Duce; citizens must serve as soldiers; and above all, citizens must never question or contradict Mussolini, because he "is always right."

Our school was strict and traditional. We were expected

to be clean and tidy. Our hands were inspected every morning. If our fingernails were dirty, our hands would be smacked with a pointer. We had to recite our arithmetic perfectly or be punished by standing in the corner facing the wall. While boys were encouraged to join youth groups where they learned their duty to their country as soldiers and warriors, girls were taught that they needed to be good mothers and to have many children. After school, the girls would converge at the seamstress' house in the neighboring village of Sassi for sewing lessons. There we would practice sewing our hems, embroider our linens, and exchange some village gossip. We tried to escape the grim reality of the outside world that was creeping up on us all.

PART THREE

Il Duce Overthrown
1942 – 1943

The war continued to escalate in Europe and North Africa. Mussolini's armies were badly supplied and poorly led. They often needed help from the Nazi forces. Defeats of the Axis troops stretched across the Mediterranean to the African continent.

In Italy, the people grew angry with Il Duce. The *partigiani,* or partisans, were part of the Italian Resistance and they battled underground against the fascist government of Mussolini alongside the Allies. The partisans and the fascist Blackshirts clashed constantly, often with innocent civilians caught in the middle. Rations, low morale and frequent defeats led to widespread dissatisfaction with Il Duce within the country.

Food rationing became widespread in Europe. In Italy, there was not enough food or supplies for the population, and people grew weary of the war. The Resistance mounted as Mussolini's fascist policies gave more money and resources to war efforts and less to the people.

In October 1942, British troops defeated the Germans and Italians in North Africa, sending the Axis forces into confused retreat. The Allied victory in North Africa was important, since it permitted the later invasion of Sicily and the Italian mainland in the summer of 1943.

In September 1943, the Fascist Grand Council, the main body of Mussolini's government, along with King Victor Emmanuel III, King of Italy, removed Benito Mussolini from power. Il Duce was imprisoned and Italian Marshall Pietro Badoglio formed a new government. In turn, the Badoglio government surrendered Italy unconditionally to the Allies.

Weary of war, most Italians were glad, but some remained loyal to Mussolini. For a short time, while all of Italy was under the new government, the villagers in Eglio were happy. Their soldiers, brothers and sons and husbands, were returning home from war. But how long would this last?

Chapter 9

JULY 1943

War came to our village slowly at first. Initially, we lulled ourselves into believing that it would be over before long. At first, the fighting had seemed far away, but as time went on, food and the most basic of necessities became more difficult to find. Shoes and clothing could not be purchased, not because of a lack of money, but because by the time the mountain towns had their pick there was nothing left. Simple everyday things like tools, lamps, and oil were hard to come by. The war effort's ravenous appetite for resources took everything away from the people.

The villagers had survived three years of war, food rations, and funerals. All the men in the village had been sent off to serve throughout Europe, Northern Africa and Russia. Letters often brought bad news about another death. When some men did come home, it was because they had been wounded or maimed. They were the lucky ones, since they came back alive.

At the beginning of the war, women and men had willingly given their gold wedding rings to aid in the war effort. For many women there was no need to keep the ring now — their men were dead. There were rumors of the horrible conditions on the Russian front, where many Eglio men had been sent. Cold and desolate prisoner of war camps awaited those who survived the brutality of the frozen Russian front.

Meanwhile, I, like everyone else, was hungry. Very hungry. There hadn't been a delivery of food supplies to Eglio for weeks. Mamma still had money and tickets in our ration books, but there was nothing left to purchase. Food and sundries were not getting to the village. Through the early winter, we relied on the food from our grandparents' plot of wheat and corn. Some dried plums and potatoes were harvested and saved. When that ran out, we had to settle for roots and scarce wild greens.

My fourteenth birthday came and went, with only a bit of wild dandelion greens, some goat's milk and cornmeal polenta for my celebration. Only Mamma and Mery were there. My other sisters were still away, working in the cities. More women were now working in the steel factories in place of the men who were off fighting at the fronts.

There was no domestic livestock left to slaughter, not even a rabbit. We had slaughtered the ones that we could manage without. Some cattle and chickens were spared for their milk and eggs. Naturally, everyone in Eglio and Sassi sold, bartered, or shared what they had. But when there was nothing left to share, we had to make do. It would be better for us soon, once we could harvest the vegetables we had planted in the spring. But for now, we ate chestnut meal. Chestnuts could always be gathered from the woods. I was getting sick of it.

The last time I had smelled the delicious aroma of bread was just before Alcide was drafted. At the time, we were only one year into the war and there were rations already. Mamma had managed to scrape together enough flour to bake a small loaf of bread. She asked Mery and me to save it for Alcide, since he was now the only one working and bringing in some money. My eyes were drawn to that little basket on the hearth. I knew that inside the neatly folded linen napkin was a heavenly, fresh-baked loaf of scrumptious bread. I also knew that I could not have any. Occasionally, I would sneak over to open up the napkin and look at the loaf, warm and fragrant. I would draw close to it and sniff the mouth-watering aroma. Then I would wrap it back up neatly, just as it was before, for Alcide. I had to keep reminding myself that it was for my brother so that he could remain strong.

I was beginning to hate Mussolini. I hated him because he was the reason for our misery. Everything had changed because of him and Hitler. I didn't understand what Il Duce wanted for our country. I wasn't sure what they were fighting for, but surely it could not be worth all this suffering. What was he gaining by having his people endure this agony for so long? I kept my thoughts to myself, of course. I knew that the fascist Blackshirts were everywhere, looking for enemies of Il Duce.

My mother told me there was an underground resistance movement against the fascists, but no one spoke out loud about it. Secret bands of partisans traveled with guns through the countryside fighting the fascists. I heard that there were partisans around Eglio, but I never saw them. Even though I couldn't possibly understand what that meant, it gave me a small sense of security and a glimmer of hope, knowing that there were groups of people who were trying to make things better for us. The Italian Resistance was growing stronger and the widespread dissatisfaction with Mussolini among the people was increasing. Though many villagers supported the resistance, in general they were frightened by the fact that when the partisans sabotaged Nazi operations, the Nazis would retaliate by taking it out on the villagers.

To make things worse, the winter seemed to drag on endlessly. The drabness and isolation of it had taken a toll on us. I had spent most of the winter evenings reading to my mother and Ida by the light of a lonely little candle. Although a robust fire was kept burning in the hearth in the kitchen, I longed for warmth and good weather to be able to wander in the woods again.

ও

Finally spring made an appearance, and I roamed the gentle slope from the fields above the village to gather up some greens. I had learned through trial and error that the farther away from the village I ventured, the more abundant the wild harvest. My old shoes were worn through to the insides and mud seeped through the holes so that it was hardly worth even wearing them anymore. It had rained heavily the previous night; the lightning and thunder still frightened me, but I was thankful that the bleak winter was over.

I looked skyward at the heavy clouds that had given way to a thin ray of sunlight on the mountains that morning. There was still a blanket of fog over Barga, one of the largest towns in the Garfagnana Valley that could be plainly seen from Eglio. The wildflowers grew once again on the hillside and the sun felt warm on my face. It gave me renewed hope.

As I approached the village I heard a commotion. Most of villagers were in the piazza and there was an uneasiness in the air. People were milling about and talking, some still in their wooden shoes from their barns. I looked for mother but didn't see her.

I approached Maria the storeowner and Eva. "What's happening, Maria?"

"Oh my goodness, Bruna…" she answered, agitated.

"It's about Mussolini's government," said Eva, her eyes wide.

"What about it?"

"Bruna!" shouted Armida from behind a group of old men. She pushed her way through. "I just came back from your grandparents' fields to tell them and your mother," she said breathlessly. "We just heard the news over the wireless… Il Duce has been overthrown. The king had him arrested."

"Is the war over then?" I looked from one person to the

next, asking no one in particular, still clutching the dandelion greens. I smiled feebly and thought that that should be a good thing.

"It means," said Alfezio, hobbling gleefully into the crowd, "that there is hope that soon this wretched war will end. There is hope that the partisans and the resistance will prevail."

I spotted my mother and ran to her from the other side of the piazza. Mery ran ahead of her to hug me. "Did you hear?" she said, a great smile on her face.

"I did. Armida just told me. This means that now our boys and men can come home." I felt an overwhelming sense of relief.

My mother, perspiring and dirty from the fields, reached us. All she could do was hold her daughters tightly among the buzz of the villagers. "Mamma, they're coming home. Aren't they?" I searched my mother's face for reassurance.

"I hope so," she said. But she seemed as apprehensive as everyone else.

"It means nothing," said Oreste, our closest neighbor, to Alfezio. "We could be worse off than before. We are wide open now. Italy is open to any country who pleases to attack it." Sadly, Oreste's intuition proved to be right.

Chapter 10

Not long after, the new Italian government under King Victor Emmanuel surrendered to the United States and Britain. And exactly eight days later Cesar returned home!

Twilight was coming and the red sun hung low in the horizon as he strode up the dirt road. He looked as though he was returning from an extended walk instead of two years at war. I looked down the road to see if Alcide was behind him as he always was. But he wasn't.

Cesar recounted how he and the other men in his regiment cheered when they heard that Mussolini and his fascist government had fallen. They abandoned their posts on the frontier and buried their uniforms so that they would not be captured by Mussolini sympathizers or by the Nazi army to be to be taken as prisoners-of-war. Many destroyed their rifles by breaking them in half over their knees so that they couldn't be used anymore. Others threw them in the river, but Cesar said he couldn't bring himself to do it. His rifle had saved his life so many times, he couldn't destroy it. He emptied his gun of any bullets and he buried the rifle deep on the slope of a hillside. That way, no one could use it to kill anyone anymore. In eight days, hiding and walking on mountain paths and back trails, he was home, but many others still were not.

Mamma wiped the tears from her eyes, as she gathered up her son and held onto him. There was applause from everyone in the village, as had become the custom to welcome the soldiers when they came home. "I'm so happy you're safe," she said, her hands gently caressed his face as if he was a little boy.

The tears came again and Cesar asked if Alcide was home yet.

"Not yet," said Mamma.

"Have you had any word?" he asked.

"Nothing." She shook her head.

"He will be home," said Cesar, convinced. "He'll be here soon. He was stationed much farther on the Greek isles."

"Yes, Mamma," Mery added. "They will all be home soon."

Cesar later told my mother and older sisters of the firefights in the harsh cold of the mountains in winter. He talked about the frenetic pace of the hikes the guards had to take in order to patrol the border. According to Cesar, the shortage of supplies and the inadequate quality of equipment made the soldiers' jobs very difficult to carry out. He tried to keep the details from me by avoiding conversations while I was around. What I was able to gather was that many of his friends didn't make it home and were buried there.

As the weeks passed, more of the men from the village returned home. Edo Guazzelli was one of them after only a brief time in the military at basic training. He had been stationed at the base in Modena, north of Florence, in the interior. Just as they were preparing to ship him out, Mussolini's government fell.

There was still no sign of Alcide.

PART FOUR

A Divided Italy
1943 – 1944

When the new leaders of the country, Marshall Pietro Badoglio and King Emmanuel III, surrendered southern Italy to the Allied forces, the Nazis wasted no time in taking northern Italy with unparalleled efficiency. Hitler's army seized control of Rome. Mussolini was freed from prison by German commandos on September 12, 1943 and became the "puppet" leader in the fascist-occupied territory with Hitler in control. Meanwhile the Allies controlled the south, attempting to defeat the Nazi regime that was gripping Europe.

Italy was now divided into two parts, with the Allies in the south and the fascists in the north. Nazi troops began to move farther into the central portion with Mussolini and his socialist republic. Now Tuscany was right between the lands occupied by the Axis and the Allies. Before long, there were German troops in the heart of the Garfagnana Valley, near the village of Eglio.

Italian citizens tried to cope with the pressures of wartime living, invasion, occupation, and the division of their country. Ordinary people continued to secretly fight in the resistance. They sought and killed fascist collaborators and hid Jews. But there were also many Italians who remained loyal to Mussolini and fascism. For the villagers of Eglio, in the path of the Nazi invaders, there was the ever-present danger of raids.

Chapter 11

When the news about the Allies landing in the south of Italy had come over the wireless, it had given us renewed hope that freedom from tyranny and chaos might be close at hand. "Italy will soon be liberated," the villagers said to each other. Patiently, we waited. The Italian Resistance continued to fight for the cause. Meanwhile life in the villages went on.

The summer passed in a climate of apprehension and uncertainty. In its wake the mountain air turned colder. Autumn allowed the trees in the woodlands and peaks surrounding the valley to show off their brilliant hues of red, orange, and yellow. The tapestry of warm colors gave an almost warming effect to the crispness of the October mountain air. It was harvest time in Eglio.

The changes in Italy had been more than I, or any other young person, could understand. "Explain the part about Il Duce being Hitler's puppet again," I would pester my brother as we worked in the fields for the harvest. We siblings did most of the work in their fields, since our nonno was very ill now and Nonna was becoming increasingly confused. Hay had to be prepared for the animals and stored in their barn in the valley below the village for the winter.

"Hitler's men brought Il Duce back to the north. The Nazis are strong here. Mussolini is our leader again," said Cesar, swinging the sling blade deftly through the hay. "Meanwhile the Allies have taken over the south of Italy. This means that our country is divided into two parts."

Though much had changed for the worse in our village that fall, life in the big cities was more dire. Because of the constant threat of looming air raids, people sought refuge in the country if they could.

Aurelia came home from her job as a cook in Pisa. When she returned, she and Dante, the son of our neighbors, Oreste and Ida, declared their engagement. They hoped to be married when the war was over. Pina came home from Livorno, where she too had been employed as a cook.

Both Pina and Aurelia told stories of Jewish families in the cities where they worked. Some already had had their rights and property snatched from them by Il Duce's fascist government. When the Nazis invaded northern Italy, things got even worse for the Jewish people. They were rounded up and sent to concentration camps where many of them were murdered.

To protect themselves, Jews were forced into hiding. Some Jewish families were given refuge by loyal Christian friends or by former employees. Others were hidden in the many crevasses and secret passages in churches, monasteries, and basilicas by priests and nuns. They fled to the countryside where farmers hid them in barns or cellars. Some Jews concealed their identities by buying false papers and calling themselves Christians to avoid being captured by the Nazis. They attended church and took communion wafers to avoid suspicion. I was horrified to think that people would be treated like this because they were of a different religion. How could evil like this triumph?

"Believe me, Bruna, it is best to be with family at times like this," Pina told me. And in spite of the horrors around us, in spite of the situation, I loved the fact that most of my family was back in Eglio. I was delighted that Pina's cooking skills could even make beets taste good.

Nora was the only one still away from home. Besides Alcide of course. Alcide was never far from anyone's mind and neither were the other men who were still missing.

Nora was still working in the orphanage in Florence. She could not bring herself to leave the children. She had let it slip that there was someone special there. His name was Mario and he was quite the urban gentleman. His family owned a pensione, a hotel, in Florence.

"Are you daydreaming, Bruna?" Cesar asked me, smiling. "Quickly, let's gather up the hay." Cesar hacked at the hay furiously. "Enough about politics. I'm growing tired of it."

"Very well." I obeyed my older brother. Still I couldn't

help but think of how life had changed from before the war. How I longed to have it back the way it was. Little did I realize we had not seen the worst of it yet.

Chapter 12

As close to us as the German soldiers were, the dreaded winter was much closer. All of us villagers had tried to store away as much of the fall harvest as possible. We knew that supplies would never get through now that the country was divided. We hid as many turnips and potatoes as possible in inconspicuous places in our homes. Under the beds, covered with blankets, in the chestnut driers in the fields, anywhere but in plain sight.

We knew that there were regiments of German soldiers based strategically in the Valley along the Serchio River. The Nazis had come boldly into Eglio and Sassi twice in the last two weeks. They had entered several homes looking for food, but had also taken valuables from the villagers.

White-faced, our friend Alice burst through our doorway

after the Nazis had left her house. "Oh, heaven help us! Those brutes forced their way into our house, ransacking everything in sight. They took all the food they could find. And then they seized our silver candlesticks, the ones that were a wedding gift." Alice wailed in despair.

"They helped themselves to my woolen blankets and good linens, too. Poor Paolo was powerless to stop them. They put a bayonet to his throat, those thieves." Mamma nodded her head in compassion.

Alice and Paolo weren't the only ones who had things taken. And the Nazis weren't only taking *things*. They were taking people, too.

When the soldiers came to Eglio, I saw them with my own eyes as I hid in my grandmother's house. Her window had a relatively clear view of the entire bottom half of the village. I saw one of the soldiers taking a villager out of his home, a bayonet pointed at his skull, his helpless wife left wailing inside the house. The sight frightened me so much I had nightmares all the next week. For the first time in my life, I did not feel safe in my own town.

The German soldiers looked for healthy men in the villages. They sent them to fight on the front lines against the enemy. Many of our men who had come back to the village from the war, now had to fight for the Nazis. Some managed to hide, but others were taken away at gunpoint.

One evening when my mother and sisters had gone to Evelina's to shell dried chestnuts, I heard my brother and some other men of the village talking in our kitchen. I was in my bedroom trying to get to sleep. But I was curious and listened to the voices of the men below.

"Those villains are sweeping through our villages and taking us like dogs off the streets," snarled Cesar. "We must do *something*."

"Not only that," said Paolo. "They take whatever they want from our homes and we can't stop them! Soon they'll take our women. I saw the way they are, the cold bastards."

I gasped when I heard this.

"I heard that they slaughter people without remorse, if they don't cooperate. They line them up against a wall three or four deep and shoot them in the head at close range to save on bullets. They hang men who are suspected of working with the partisans along the road leading to the village," cried Demetrio, angrier than I had ever heard him. "Children and babies are bayoneted to teach everyone a lesson!"

I felt sick to my stomach. Silently, I crept out of bed and tiptoed over to the top of the stairs and watched the men below as they talked and smoked.

"We may not be able to fight them, but we must protect ourselves," responded Cesar.

"But how?" asked Oreste.

"They have guns," growled Edo. "We have nothing."

"We have our brains," replied Cesar. "We can use our brains to outsmart them."

"They are an army," snapped Edo motioning his disgust. "How can we? If they see me and anyone else who can walk, they'll take us. They're devils!"

"They can't take us if they don't find us," said Cesar.

"Come on, Cesar. We can't hide in the shadows forever," said Enrico. "We have work to do."

"Animals to tend and feed, we must go to our barns and storage houses…"

"Gather food, plant and harvest our fields…"

"Yes, yes, I understand, but, thank goodness, they are not here all the time," said Cesar, exhaling cigarette smoke. "We need to hide only when they're coming."

"But how will we know when they're coming?" asked Paolo.

"We need to find a way of warning everyone," said Cesar, thinking out loud.

Demetrio snapped his fingers. "My house is almost in the middle of the village. If I keep an eye out for the Germans, maybe I could warn the village somehow."

"How can you warn everyone in Eglio including those who are working in the fields?" asked Paolo. "Your house can't be seen from all points."

"No, Paolo, maybe not from *your* house," said Cesar to Oreste slowly. "*Your* house wouldn't be right, but Evelina's would be!"

A spontaneous chorus of "Evelina's house!" resounded in the little kitchen.

"Quickly, let's go now!" said Demetrio gravely. "We've got to get this sorted out tonight before the Nazis come back."

In what seemed like an instant, they were all gone. They had run out the door into the night, I guessed to Evelina's. I was by myself, praying that they had thought of a way to protect themselves and the others. I wondered what they could possibly be planning. How would they get word to an entire village when the Germans were coming?

Now that they were gone, it was so quiet. I shivered and reached for the blanket at the foot of my bed, and wrapped it around my shoulders. I crept downstairs and pulled a chair close to the fire in the hearth, stoking it to enliven the flames. I watched the flames dance in the hearth, yellow, orange, and white blending together and then parting. I thought of Alcide and wondered what he was doing now. He was one of the soldiers who had not returned home. I prayed he was still alive somewhere.

The embers were bright and the smell of burning wood was comforting. Although I was afraid to be in the house by myself, I was beginning to feel terribly sleepy near the warm fire. My head began to nod and my eyelids grew heavy. Giving in to sleep, finally, I arose and went to my own bed. For once, sleep was victorious over fear.

Chapter 13

The next morning came quickly. Although it was still relatively dark outside, Paolo and Alice's rooster down the lane crowed like it was set by an alarm clock. The January days were short and cold and I felt it in my bones that the fire had died during the night. Turning over, I saw that mother was still asleep. The one lone candle in the room cast a long shadow over our quilted covers sewn lovingly together with a variety of fabric scraps. Then I remembered. The women had all been at Evelina's when the men left our house in a rush. Mamma must know about the plan they came up with.

"Mamma," I said, nudging her gently. "Mamma, wake up."

"Yes…what?" she murmured, sleepily. She turned her head slightly to look at me.

"Last night, Mamma, what happened at Evelina's? Did the men come up there?"

She yawned and gave me a sly smile. "You'll see today, when you climb the steps up to the top of the ridge to go to grandmother's. You can see if you go to the fields below the road, too."

I couldn't wait to see the plan they had hatched last night.

&

"How very clever," said Armida later that day. We friends were all together looking up at Evelina's kitchen window from the street below.

"Yet perfectly simple and not in the least suspicious," agreed Beppina.

"And the blanket can be seen from nearly everywhere in the village and the fields," I boasted, filled with pride that I had been present at the moment the plan had been hatched.

Mamma had explained it to me earlier that day. "Do you see the white blanket over the sill of the window?" She pointed to the innocuous looking bedspread.

"Yes?" I answered, a bit puzzled. "You mean Evelina's coverlet is going to protect us from the Nazi soldiers?"

Mamma laughed and shook her head. "It's not the blanket. It's what it means."

"What does it mean?"

"Someone will always be on watch at Evelina's house, either she or one of the men. From her house you can see the road, right to the bend around the hillside of Campi della Regina, leading up to the village and the entire valley below. Everyone working in the valley can see her kitchen window, which faces the farming fields. If she, or whoever is on watch, spots anything suspicious coming around the bend, they will hang a red blanket outside on the windowsill to warn us. We will know this is the signal to hide in whatever we are closest to — in barns, drying huts, the woods. The men will stay hidden until the soldiers leave. When it is safe, a white blanket is the signal that all is clear. Right now, we can see the white blanket, which means that all is well."

A grin crept across my face as I repeated the details to my friends. Then I drew my lips together and became more serious, vowing to myself that I would be strong and brave. "So keep an eye out for it," I explained, "when you're working or about the village. If you see red, then warn anyone who may not be able to see it. Spread the word."

As the weeks unfolded, the plan worked well and the villagers were comforted by the fact that they had a plan that might give them some control over their lives. Yes, we were at the mercy of the Nazis. We experienced fear whenever soldiers came into our village. But the red blanket was a small measure of victory that kept us going for a while. The men were vigilant in their look-out duties and the plan was hailed as a triumph. It gave us the chance to hide our loved ones, our food, and our belongings.

One night, Cesar gathered up the empty steamer trunk that had held their clothes on the voyage back from Brazil.

Cesar and my older sisters hiked to the family barn in the shadowy fields below the town. The trunk was heavy, but Cesar was strong and he held it securely on his back.

Earlier that day, Mamma had carefully gathered up all her treasured belongings and placed them in bundles. "Here," she said, with determination. "Wrap fabric around all the breakable items for protection."

In the bundles, she placed the matrimonial sheets and blankets that she had embroidered as a bride, along with her best linen tablecloth sets with matching napkins stitched with her initials. Among the cloths, my sisters hid some of our grandmother's belongings from her days in the hotel business, such as silver candlesticks, flatware, and crystal. We had to hide them from my nonna who would never have parted with them otherwise. I was certain that Nonna wasn't even sure there was a war going on. Her dementia grew more severe as the months passed and Cesar was constantly having to retrieve her from wandering in the woods.

We worked at night under the dark sky so as not to attract attention. My sisters and mother carried the treasures balanced on their head and on their backs. They hiked back and forth from Poggetti to the barn in the valley below. Cesar neatly cleared the dirt floor of hay. Then he set to work digging the hole. Once all of our possessions were safely laden in the trunk, my sisters took small spades and shovels and helped him dig a hole deep enough to bury the trunk.

The donkey was moved outside so it wouldn't be spooked and the chickens and rabbits remained in their pens as Cesar and we women worked quickly to finish before the sun came up. When the hole was large enough, they lined the bottom with dry, crunchy hay and then lowered the bursting trunk into it. Once it was securely in place, they stuffed hay along the sides and filled it to the top to absorb excess moisture. Cesar had fashioned a lid with barn boards and they placed it carefully over the top. This was covered with heavily patted down dirt, followed by a thick layer of hay. No one could possibly see the hole underneath. The donkey pen was moved over the top and the soil from the hole was carried out with baskets and pails and thrown far from the barn so that it would not be obvious.

Our family's treasures were safe for the time being.

Chapter 14

Winter had pulled a heavy gray blanket over the skies above the village. The Christmas of 1943 would be another lean holiday. Cesar cut a little tree in the woods and brought it to the house. Mery and I decorated it with some homemade trinkets and dried fruit from our grandparents' orchards. There were no gifts under the tree. In our home, gifts were exchanged on the Epiphany in January, as was the Italian custom. We knew that there would be nothing save for the socks that Mamma had knitted for each of us from the wool that we had sheared from Nonno's sheep earlier that year. The woolen socks were a bit scratchy, but they were warm and kept my feet cozy at night.

Christmas Mass was a solemn event and our Christmas feast was simple: chicken, potatoes, greens, and some dried fruit for sweets afterwards. My family ate in silence, the specter of Alcide's absence never far from anyone's mind. At one point, despite putting on a brave face, Mamma's eyes grew mournful. Alcide's place at the table was empty, and so was Nora's. It felt like a huge piece of our family was missing that year, even though there were six of us around the modest meal. Everyone knew Nora was safe, but no one could possibly guess what had become of our brother. This was too much for Mother to bear.

"Mamma, don't cry," pleaded Pina. "The fact that we don't know is good, isn't it Cesar? He could be alive somewhere, hiding."

Cesar set down his fork and wiped his mouth. "I think so," he answered without raising his eyes. "He can be strong and very resourceful."

"Yes, Cesar is right," said Aurelia, draping an arm around our mother. "He'll be back. As loud and boisterous as ever." She forced a laugh.

Mamma wiped her eyes. Even with this heaviness in her heart, this great sadness, she maintained her dignity and strength. She held up her head. "Wherever he is, I pray that he knows we are holding him in our hearts. *Buon natale*, Merry Christmas."

"Buon natale," we repeated. Outside, it smelled like snow, but in our kitchen, the fire in the hearth burned warm and bright.

Chapter 15

Snow fell on the mountain peaks like sugar dusting a *panettone*. In Eglio, food became ever more scarce in the winter months. Food rations had been in place now for four years and some of the younger children could not remember a time when the cupboards and pantries were full.

The war raged on, its tentacles reaching into every part of our lives. January gave way to the harsh winds of February, its skies cold and gray, and soon March with its heavy rain was upon us. The arrival of another spring was just weeks away and still there was no end in sight to the war. The hope that the Allies would soon bring liberation faded.

I was maturing and becoming a young woman before my mother's eyes. Next month, in April, I would turn fifteen. My schooling would soon finish and in normal times, I would be searching for work. But times were not normal. So my friends and I kept busy, sewing, and gathering food from wherever we could find it. We read and told stories and talked of what we'd do when life returned to normal.

"What will you do first, when the war ends?" whispered Armida. It was just before Easter and we were seated in the front pews of our little church.

"Let me think," mused Beppina, her chin resting on her hands folded over the back of our pew. Her blonde hair spilled out from under her headscarf and cascaded over her shoulders. We were in church but not entirely engrossed in our Easter novena, a special prayer said in the days leading up to Easter. "Maybe, I'll go to Castelnuovo when the marketplace resumes. I want to buy new boots, the ones lined with fur. And they need to have fancy heels and shiny buckles. What about you, Zelinda?" Zelinda was Beppina's older sister.

"Do you really need to ask?" she responded with a glare. "I want Alcide to come back safe and sound." Her voice was impatient and her eyes began to well up. She looked up to the altar again, her hands clasped and continued to pray.

"Of course, Zelinda," said Beppina apologetically, surprised at her own insensitivity. "I'm so sorry." Beppina turned to Armida. "What about you?" she whispered with a guilty side glance.

Armida thought hard, her dark eyes narrowing in deliberation. "Well, of course I want my brother back, too." Lino, her brother was stationed at the Russian front, along with Edo's brother, Mario. "I want him home safe. Once he is home, I will go to the marketplace to buy a new dress to celebrate." She smiled and looked at the cherubs painted on the ceiling. "Yes, a new dress. Mine are all in tatters." She looked at the dress she was wearing and ran a hand over the hem, a patch of strategically place fabric sewn carefully onto the side of it.

"And you, Bruna?" asked Armida.

I swallowed and thought of my brother. And then to the turnips and potatoes I had for lunch. "Alcide, of course," I said solemnly. "And after that, I'd want to celebrate by going to a restaurant." My face almost reluctantly burst into a broad smile as I recalled the last time I had dined in a *trattoria* in Castelnuovo. My nonno and nonna had done business in Castelnuovo, selling their cheeses, vegetables, and fruits from their farm to the merchants. I would tag along sometimes and they would treat me to lunch. I remembered it well. The bumpy donkey ride on the narrow dirt road below Sassi was lengthy and daunting.

"Sounds divine," sighed Armida. Then she suddenly turned serious and with a quick motion she turned around, kneeling hard on the wooden knee rests. We knew instinctively what that meant. The priest was approaching and it would not be appropriate to be conducting a frivolous conversation in church on Good Friday.

"Good evening, girls," whispered Don Turriani. He was kindly and older with a ruddy complexion and a great red nose.

"Good evening, Father," we quietly responded in unison.

We assumed our reverent postures, kneeling with hands folded, our rosaries tightly clasped through our fingers.

"I must say, it is highly refreshing to see such respect from the youth of the parish," he said thoughtfully, as he strode to the front of the church.

We smiled up at him. "Thank you, Father," we said once more in unison. We watched as he proceeded to the vestment chamber. Edo Guazzelli was there, as usual, helping the priest in some way or other. He was on a ladder patching some water damage over the frescoes behind the altar. The winter had been a harsh one on the inside of the chapel as well as out.

Edo deftly stepped down from the ladder. Now that the re-plastering was finished, Don Turriani would re-paint the scene as he always did. This little church was his pride. I marveled that he had, in fact, painted the entire scene in the chapel, modeled after the frescoes in the churches in Rome. Still kneeling with hands clasped, I watched Edo while he put away the last of his tools. He went to the back room and exchanged a few words with the priest, after which he emerged with his jacket. As he walked toward us, he glanced at me and winked almost imperceptibly. I felt my face burn and I was sure it had turned a crimson red.

Beppina and Armida turned their heads slightly to watch the handsome young man leave, and then their attention turned to me and my beet-red face.

"What's the matter?" asked Beppina, her hand on my shoulder.

"N-Nothing," I stuttered, my eyes to the ground.

"Shh!" hissed one of the women in the pew behind us.

Zelinda turned around and mouthed, "Quiet!" Then she saw me, flustered and red. "What?" she asked softly.

"Nothing," I mouthed back. I felt a tingling in my stomach and my ears felt warm. I was becoming a young woman and Edo Guazzelli had winked at me. One of the most handsome young men in the village, winked at *me*. We had always been friends. And he was a friend of my brothers. We were all friends in our little village, but sometimes things changed. I had seen it before. He had winked at me and only me. I was flattered and confused. Nature waits for no one and young girls grow into young women, whether there is war or not.

PART FIVE

Caught on the Gothic Line
1944

By June 1944, the Allies had landed on the Normandy beaches, and all of France would soon be liberated. In September 1944, the Allies pushed into Eastern Europe, liberating Poland and other occupied Eastern European countries. It was the beginning of the end for Nazi Germany.

In Italy, the Allies had landed in the port of Anzio on January 22, 1944. The Allies then captured Monte Cassino, an important German stronghold, and in early June 1944, Allied forces entered Rome. The Allies continued to crush the Nazis in town after Italian town: Elba, Assisi, Perugia, and finally Florence. Gradually they tried to make their way northward.

Not wanting the Allies to advance farther north, the Nazis created "the Gothic Line." It extended for more than 185 miles

(300 km) and cut across the Italian mainland from east to west. It traversed Garfagnana, crossed Tuscany, and cut through to Bologna.

The Nazis used the natural landscape of the Italian Alps to their advantage, creating strongholds through the Apennine Mountains. They also used Italian villagers to build walls in pockets of the Gothic Line, made of wood, rock, steel, and reinforced concrete. Nazis also forced villagers to build machine gun nests, bunkers, anti-tank ditches, and deadly minefields.

Allied forces battled valiantly to break these defenses, but were unable to get beyond the Gothic Line. Meanwhile, Italian partisans tried to disrupt Nazi defenses from the mountains and the villages. Now Eglio, on the Gothic Line, found itself in the center of one of the last fortified Nazi fronts.

Chapter 16

SPRING 1944

Spring was a busy time for the farmers in Eglio. We continued to work just outside the village on Nonna and Nonno's terraced hillside farm, abundant with wheat, corn and tender fruit trees. All able members of our family, those who were at home, were involved in keeping up our food supply.

When we weren't working in the fields, we kept a constant vigil and listened to the wireless, hoping for further news about the war. On the radio, there were reports of the Allies making their way north from Anzio. After the long months of winter, they were advancing fast. We heard frightening reports of massacres and atrocities, of unspeakable evil being carried out by Nazi forces all over Europe. A mass execution took place in Rome in March 1944 by Nazi troops as punishment for a partigiani attack in the city. In spite of these reports, the people tried to maintain some form of normality in Eglio, but it was hard not to be afraid. We worried that something terrible like this would happen to us.

The British and Americans continued to move north from Florence in August, working their way up to Northern Tuscany through the Apennines. They finally came to the town of Barga, just below us, and set up a base there. I didn't know at the time that this was called the Gothic Line.

Nazis outposts were falling and their regiments retreated farther into Northern Tuscany. Unfortunately for us, as the Allies got closer, the Nazis began moving into the mountains. Our mountains — where we grew our food, fed our livestock, and raised our families — were being used by the Nazi butchers to protect themselves.

There were whispers of further carnage as the Germans grew more frustrated and angry with the resistance fighters. In August, in the community of Sant' Anna, Nazi soldiers brutally murdered the entire village in cold blood — almost six hundred all together — in retaliation for actions from partisan fighters. In the village of Patule, close to two hundred civilians were killed for the same reason. There was word that the men were hung with barbed wire. These horrific reports of Nazi atrocities, coupled with more bombings and gunfire in the distance, resulted in much anxiety in our village. The Nazis were almost upon us and we grew more frightened as each day passed.

The people of Eglio had a good vantage point and could

see the entire valley. Evelina's red blanket was well used, as Nazi troops were seen more often in and around Molazzana, a village more than halfway up the mountain between Barga and Eglio. Through the spring and summer, our village was under constant alert. Then, one day in September, our dreadful indisputable destiny presented itself.

છ

As my family and I worked in the fields, a great ruckus came from the road — the sound of carriage wheels traveling at a furious pace on the pebbly surface. It was Demetrio. He had left earlier that day with his mule and carriage to go to Molazzana to barter some supplies. He spotted Mamma in the fields and he waved his hat, motioning for us to come down to the road. As we hurried down the hill to greet him we could see that he was upset. He stopped the carriage abruptly, dismounted, and ran to meet up with us.

"I just came from the cross roads to enter Molazzana," he said as he breathed heavily and wiped his brow with his sleeve. "The Nazi soldiers are there. On their way up." He gasped another breath. "And they are burying land mines all along the side of the road…where truck tires would go…on the sides."

"Mother of God!" Mamma cupped her hands over her mouth.

"Those bastards!" hissed Cesar.

"Landmines?" My voice quivered. "Mamma, what will we do?"

"How many soldiers?" asked Aurelia, her eyes wide.

"Dozens from what I could see," replied Demetrio. "Maybe more."

I swallowed, though my mouth felt dry, like parchment. "Do you mean they are coming here to Eglio?" I felt sick to my stomach.

Mamma grabbed my arm and hugged me. "Shh. It's all right," she said, her tone less than convincing. I wanted to believe her, but common sense made me think otherwise. I felt my eyes dart from my brother to Demetrio to my sisters, searching for answers.

"How far up are they?" asked Cesar. "How much time do you think we have?" He took off his hat and wiped his brow as he began walking up the hill.

"When I saw them, at the rate they were burying those mines, they'll be here probably the day after tomorrow. Maybe earlier if they send an advance guard."

"That's it then," said Cesar sternly. "The front is moving up the mountain through Eglio. We need to tell everyone now!"

"I'll go ahead," said Demetrio, his voice trembling. He turned on his heel, stumbling a little in his haste. Swiftly, he mounted the buggy and clicked his tongue at the mule as he snapped the reins. In an instant, he was off, his cart jogging wildly toward the village.

Grabbing his sickle, Cesar ran ahead of everyone, his pace quickening to reach the footpath back to Eglio.

I ran after him, my blood pumping wildly through my veins.

I looked back at my mother and sisters as they scaled the trellised hillside. Pina and Aurelia struggled up the steep hill, grasping at the ground for leverage while helping Mamma along, their worn out shoes digging into the red earth.

"Cesar, what are we going to do?" I scampered alongside him like a puppy.

"I don't know," said Cesar. His voice betrayed his alarm. "But we have to spread the word." He stopped suddenly and took my arm, jerking me to a stop. "But no matter what, you need to stay away from them — the Nazis. Do you understand? Stay as far away as you can. You need to stay safe."

I bobbed my head up and down in quick, short bursts. I couldn't find the words to answer him. His nervousness increased *my* fear. My brave and stalwart brother, afraid? I had never seen him this way. We scrambled upward on the hillside to the footpath where Evelina's house was in plain view. I figured that Demetrio had made it into town and delivered the crushing news because Evelina's red blanket hung from the window for all to see.

We went directly to Ferrari's bar, which shouldered both the square and the main avenue. Ferrari's wireless was delivering the news to the huddled villagers. The Allies had made it to the Gothic Line. Our little town and all its people were now in the middle of the only front left defended by the Nazis in Italy.

Chapter 17

In late September 1944, an envoy of Nazi soldiers rode into town. There was no need for Evelina's red blanket as the entire town was now on high alert. The soldiers stopped their three vehicles in the town piazza, adjacent to Ferrari's bar.

The townspeople scattered and ran to take cover in their hiding places. Some hid in their basements, some in their barns, some in their chestnut drying huts. The men had all gone into hiding the day before at the urging of their families. The rest of the village expected to be hidden by the time the soldiers finally made it up to Eglio, but the soldiers arrived sooner than we expected. We had hoped that they would pass through and proceed on over the ridge and into the next town. But it was not to be.

The soldiers dismounted from their trucks, rifles ready for any possible conflict. The only townspeople visible were our frightened elders or women shielding their children and running away.

Pina and Aurelia and I were at the fountain, filling pails with water before the soldiers rolled in. We dropped our pails when we heard the trucks coming and ran to hide under the archway passage in the middle of town just behind the fountain. As we stood still, I peered from the archway and saw two jeeps filled with the soldiers.

"Listen, everyone!" shouted someone in Italian as he and the others descended from one of the jeeps. He was the only one not in uniform, and he held up his hands to show that he bore no weapons. "There is no need to fear the soldiers. They will not hurt you if you cooperate with them." He spoke with a northern Italian dialect and his tone was placating rather than threatening. He was obviously an Italian guide and interpreter, working for the Nazis.

"Pina, what do think they want with us?" I whispered.

"I don't know, but stay close to me." Pina gingerly reached her hand around to me as I hid behind her. She gently pushed me against the wall so that I couldn't be seen. I closed my eyes and rested against the cool masonry of the archway. My heart pounding, I continued to listen intently.

"The officers and soldiers in the Fuehrer's Army stationed to this front are on their way to your village. They will be using your homes as lodging and will require your assistance with other necessary preparations." As he spoke, the soldiers remained standing with guns in hand.

As we listened, we were unaware that the soldiers from the other jeep had walked up to the archway behind us. I heard a harsh bark from behind and recognized it as German. My sisters and I whirled around simultaneously to see four Nazi soldiers with their bayoneted rifles pointed at us. We had been so focused on the soldiers in the piazza that we didn't hear the others approaching. My heart felt as though it would jump out of my chest. I had never been so close to German soldiers before. I can recall to this day every detail of their uniforms, the color of the stitch work, their stature and their faces.

A short soldier snapped at us from the back, his voice shrill. My sisters and I stood there petrified. I was closest to him, so close that I saw the spittle fly out of his mouth as he shouted. His eyes were steel gray and watery. He couldn't have been older than twenty, if that. We had not the slightest notion of what he could be saying.

Then the taller one shouted something, obviously growing frustrated that we didn't understand. His tone was angry and urgent, his teeth like a wolf's fangs.

"*Pattat, pattat!*" The little one shouted again. In a mixed moment of sheer terror and reflex, I felt an uncontrollable urge to laugh at the little man as he yelled in his German accent. I could not suppress a huge snort and I laughed out loud before I could catch and stop myself. Aurelia and Pina shushed me and Pina slapped me across the mouth.

The little soldier oozed fury, his almost transparent skin flushing red with anger. He pursed his lips and walked toward us. I was terrified, thinking of what he might do to me. He thrust the barrel of his gun at me and continued his tirade, yelling in German. I still didn't understand what he was saying and that appeared to frustrate him even further. He proceeded to rap me on the head quite forcefully with the tip of his rifle. The other soldiers behind him walked to his side, still pointing their weapons.

From the corner of my eye, I saw Pina nodding in an exaggerated fashion and repeating, "She is a child. She didn't mean it. She is sorry. Please forgive her." The short soldier continued to shout at me. His words were like bullets. Aurelia worked her way in front and tried to move me behind her to shield me from his wrath.

In a moment of pure instinct, I turned and ran. It did not occur to me that they could have fired at point blank range and killed me on the spot. My resolve to be strong and resilient had evaporated. All I could think of was to run to my mother. Mamma was at Vincenzo's house. His house was in the valley beyond the village, hidden from view off the main road. It was the safest house in the village because of its location and my family was always welcome there.

Run to Mamma. The panic was rising up and my throat felt tight. My breath came in short bursts. My wooden shoes were slippery on the cobblestones and in my frenzy to get to the safe house I slipped and fell on my knees, scraping the skin. My destination was in front of me now and I burst through the door, letting my emotion pour out. Mamma was the first to reach me and scooped me up in her arms.

"Bruna!" she gasped. "What is it?" She held my face in her hands, and noticed the blood running down to my ankles from my scraped knees. "What happened?"

As I held onto her, I could see other people beyond the alcove in the adjacent room. Alfezio, Vincenzo and his family, Ida and Oreste, their son Dante, my brother Cesar and Mery. A horrible realization struck me. If the soldiers were following me, I would have brought them straight to all these people that I loved.

"They're in town…" I finally choked out. I could barely form the words. "They have guns." My breath wouldn't steady itself as I gasped for oxygen.

Vincenzo stepped into the alcove to the door. Behind me I heard a thump and clunk as he locked it.

Cesar was close behind mother. He was already at my side. He took my hands and held them to his chest. "Bruna, just breathe," he said calmly. "Look at me." He grasped my skinny arms in his strong hands and tried to get me to focus as I gasped for breath. My big brother's voice was comforting. "Stay calm now."

I nodded and did as I was told. The cadence of his words was soothing. My sobs waned and I stopped gasping. I nodded to him that I was all right. That was when we heard the distinct clicking of boots outside. I will never forget that sound, like the ominous regular tolling of the church funeral bell.

There was a silent pause and then the locked door

splintered and burst open, its wood unable to withstand the force of a booted foot. The German soldiers who had chased me were now positioned on the threshold, their rifles pointed into the center of the room.

One of them began shouting at us again, pointing his rifle. He stepped in as if he were entering an enemy bunker. The others spilled in.

A growly command came from a soldier with ice-blue eyes. He strode over to Vincenzo, who was closest to the door, and poked his ribs with the barrel of his gun, motioning for him to raise his hands. The old man winced and complied.

"Hands in the air!" Everyone finally understood. We all put our hands up.

"Please," said Cesar raising his hands and trying to contain his obvious fury. "Don't hurt the women."

The one with the blue eyes marched forcefully over to Cesar and hit him in the stomach with the butt of his rifle. Cesar doubled over in agony, gasping in pain. Everyone cried out. The soldier then raised his knee and hit Cesar in the face as he was doubled over. Blood spurted out of his nose, but still he said nothing. His face was twisted and covered in blood.

"Please don't hurt my son!" Mamma knelt on the floor and clasped her hands, begging for mercy. She looked at the soldier with the ice-blue eyes. Mery, tears running down her face, held onto mother's shoulders, trying to pull her back.

"Stop, Mamma," she whispered. "They'll hurt you, too."

I was helpless, trembling behind Mamma, holding onto her for fear that they would hit her.

A soldier who had walked in after the rest seemed different from the others. He stood taller and spoke calmly. He was cleaner and his uniform was fancier.

Two of the soldiers walked over, pulled Cesar to his feet and shoved him in the direction of the door. Fear overtook Mamma and she wailed. She threw herself at the feet of the soldier who had just entered and held her clasped hands up to him.

"Mercy, please, I beg you," Mamma cried.

I cried silently, my hands over my ears, trying to muffle my mother's words. But Mamma's pleading fell on deaf ears. The soldiers began prodding all the men with their rifles, pushing them out the door. The calm soldier looked at the crying women in the room. We were all worried that we would never see Cesar or the other men alive again. I held on tightly to my mother.

"All you women," said the calm one in broken Italian, "come with us."

Still weeping, we did as we were told, not making eye contact, too afraid to even give the soldiers a sideways glance. I prayed that they would spare us. I prayed that the tall one wasn't being calm just to trick us into submission. "Mamma," I whispered, tears streaming down my face. My mother's arms were like wings over my shoulders and Mery's. She had regained her composure.

"Hush," she replied under her breath. "Everything will be all right. They won't hurt us. We are not important enough to them." For the first time in my life, I didn't believe my mother.

Chapter 18

At gunpoint from Vincenzo's house, we women were led back into the piazza. Now the piazza was filled with women and children who had been rounded up from all over the village. The men, except for the elderly, were gone. I saw my friends with their sisters and mothers, clinging to one another.

"Bruna, look for your sisters," Mamma said. "Help me find them."

I scanned the piazza toward the valley overlooking Barga and then north over to Sassi. All I could see was more soldiers coming. More of them in their mossy green uniforms and dirty boots, some walking, some riding in trucks bearing huge artillery gunners. There were hundreds of them now, not dozens as Demetrio had first estimated.

I looked south, over to the steep incline toward the cemetery. That was when I saw Aurelia and Pina struggling with Nonna who was extremely agitated. She was waving her cane threateningly at the German soldiers, upset at having been pulled from her home at this hour of the day.

"Look, Mamma," I said and pointed to them. They looked as bewildered and frightened as everyone else around them. "There are the other girls! Let's try and get to them!"

"Are you mad?" whispered Mery. "They'll shoot us all."

"They're busy gathering everyone up," I said. "Besides, I want to help with Nonna and find out whether Nonno is safe."

Very slowly and cautiously, we nudged our way through the crowd. Some of the soldiers were still coming into the piazza with newly rounded-up villagers, their hands hoisted over their heads. There was a low hum of whimpers and cries in the air.

We were just a few steps away from joining the rest of our family when the neatly dressed commander began to speak in German again. When we finally reached my sisters and nonna, we discreetly held hands and kept our eyes downcast, so we would not draw too much attention to ourselves. We also tried to keep Nonna calm.

The Italian interpreter translated what the commander was saying. "Listen, everyone," he repeated. "You will not be harmed if you co-operate." He looked at the crowd, making eye contact as if to assure us that he was being truthful. "The officers will take their positions in the homes they feel are suitable to their needs. Obviously, those families whose houses are occupied by the soldiers will need to stay elsewhere.

"The commander requires women to cook for the officers. All food in and around the village will be seized. The women will also wash the soldiers' clothing." He continued to scan the crowd of women. "Those of you who are chosen will go with the soldiers. They will show you where you will be working."

Then the commander took on a distinctively more severe tone. "You will not be allowed to leave here, and no person shall be allowed to enter the village. We have placed landmines on all southerly routes to and from Eglio." At this, everyone looked at one another in disbelief. Now we would be totally isolated.

"Cooks, here!" shouted the short soldier. He waved his rifle toward the railing of the piazza closest to the bar.

"Those he selects will be in charge of preparing meals daily for the officers. You will gather in that area," translated the Italian.

The soldier began selecting the cooks with the tip of his bayonet. Pina and Aurelia were amongst the first to be chosen and they hurriedly moved to the chosen spot.

"Washers, here!" The commander pointed to several of the older women, including Mamma.

Mery and I held our mother's arms. "Don't worry. You can let go," Mamma said, as she wiped her cheeks with her hands, her eyes red from crying. "Do as they say. It's our only hope." She took our hands in hers and kissed them and then took Nonna's hand firmly. "I'm just over here." She walked away, taking my grandmother with her. I could feel the panic in my stomach rising.

"Cook's helpers, here!" said the little one, snarling out another order. With this, he waved his rifle at us, along with some of the other younger girls and directed us beside the cooks. Several of my friends were in the group.

"You will help in the kitchen," said the interpreter.

Mery started moving toward the area where he pointed his rifle. I felt as though I was rooted to the spot. "No," I whispered almost imperceptibly. "No."

"Bruna," Mery hissed under her breath. "Move. Now!"

"No, I won't. They're going to kill us."

"Didn't you hear Mamma? Do as they say." Mery grasped my arm roughly, forcing me over. I could see my sisters, silently trying to signal us toward them. That was when the little soldier who had previously smacked me on the head with his rifle strode over.

"You again? There!" *Tap, tap, tap* went the rifle barrel on my head. "There!" he bellowed in broken Italian. I shut my eyes and winced at the sharp pain of the cold metal making contact with my skull. I heard my mother cry out from the distance. Others around me gasped.

The commander, amused, walked over to observe the scene. He nodded to the interpreter to attend and he was there in a flash. The commander smiled slightly as he gave instructions in German. The interpreter turned to me and said calmly, "He does not want you to be afraid. He only wants you to peel potatoes."

The commander nodded for me to go. Mery took hold of my arm. "Just do what I do," whispered Mery. "Follow me, Bruna."

Chapter 19

We were directed, again at gunpoint, to one of the larger houses in the village, the one belonging to the Ferrari family. The house was attached to Ferrari's bar and ideal for the soldiers since it had a large enough space for all the officers to dine together. In addition, it had an excellent vantage point into the center of the village. Pina, Aurelia, and I were led to the kitchen.

As our group was ushered to the little courtyard in the back, I caught sight of some of the supplies lying randomly on the tables. The soldiers were shouting orders at some of the village men, directing them with crates and containers of food. Baskets full of meats, greens, and potatoes were lined up on the scrubbed tables. Lard and oil were stored in containers brought by the soldiers. We had seen nothing like this bounty in our village for quite some time.

On the huge stove and in the sinks were the bar's pots, used to fix simple meals for the once busy village bar and *osteria*. They had sat idle for a long time because of the food shortage. I thought that if they were alive they would have forgotten their purpose.

When we entered the courtyard, we saw an overflowing sack of potatoes propped up between two half barrels in the center of the yard. There were a few chairs and some knives thrown on the table in the middle.

"*Pattat, pattat,*" stuttered one of the soldiers, motioning toward the sacks with his rifle.

"Of course," I whispered. "He means *patata* — potatoes. They want us to peel the potatoes."

Eva was the first to cautiously walk to a chair and pull it up to the table. She picked up one of the knives and looked guardedly at the officers. Then she selected a potato from the sack and began to peel it.

Armida was the next to take a knife and begin peeling. Mery soon surrendered to their commands. I was the only one left. I stood in the courtyard doorway. I hated to think that we were forced to help feed these loathsome creatures. But I knew the choice was to cooperate or die. They would hurt me if I refused. The girls looked at me as they peeled.

"Come," murmured Mery through clenched teeth. "Come here, *now*."

I looked at the guards. One of them lit a cigarette and sat down. He took a long drag from his cigarette, blew out the smoke, and then loudly pulled back the safety lock on his rifle. The sound startled me and made me jump. The soldier guffawed loudly over my reaction. I took my place at the cutting table.

&

Late that afternoon, everyone went home — everyone who had a home to go to. Those whose houses were taken over by the German officers had to stay with others in the village. As for the men, there was no use hiding anymore. All were found. Those who were strong enough were made to work on building bunkers for the soldiers. They had to dig deep fortified holes in the Bora valley behind the village, the best place to avoid an enemy attack from Barga.

That night, Cesar made it home, too. I was so grateful that he was unharmed, though he was still bloody from the beating earlier in the day. When he entered our little kitchen at Poggetti, I hugged him for a long time.

He told us that the soldiers had taken him and other villagers to begin digging up the beautiful green Bora meadow, which opened to the valley behind Eglio. These ugly holes would become the foundation for the Nazi's bunkers to be used for their protection.

Our family gathered around the kitchen table, but there was only chestnut polenta, a few potatoes, and some boiled dandelion greens for dinner. It was a paltry spread compared to the feast we had prepared for the Nazis that afternoon.

"They took the wireless radio from the bar, too," Pina said in a low voice. She looked tired. "Someone said they took it up near the Palazzo." The *Palazzo* wasn't really a palace. The people just called it that because it was the biggest house in Eglio. The soldiers had taken it as their headquarters because it was in the middle of the village overlooking the valley, surrounded by other houses. Strategically, it was a good location to avoid shelling I would later find out.

"Now we have no way of knowing what's happening in the world around us," said Cesar.

"Just be thankful that we are all here, safe and alive." Mamma's voice had an unusual edge. "There are others who have suffered a worse fate." With that statement, everyone around the table hushed and bowed their heads, continuing to choke down the meager dinner in silence.

Cesar was the first to finish. It didn't take a man very long to finish this meal, especially after digging giant holes all day.

Chapter 20

So it went for days. Fear, dread, and the daily drudgery of having to cater to our captors drove our existence. We were constantly uneasy and afraid of infuriating the soldiers. We were free to move about the village, but we had to adhere to our dusk curfew and couldn't leave Eglio's boundaries at all. This had terrible consequences for those in our community who were sick and needed more medical care than the villagers could provide.

"Edo told me that his father is very ill," Cesar said from his place at the table. "He's weaker than ever and in a lot of pain."

"Poor, Enrico," sighed Mamma. "Your nonno is much worse, too. I should visit them again very soon to see if I can do anything for them."

"Do you think that the German soldiers will let you go to their house?" Mery asked.

"I *must* go. We have to look after our sick."

"I'll go with you, Mamma," I offered.

"I will, too," echoed Mery.

It would have been so easy if the Nazis weren't here. We would just take our sick people through the back roads to the hospital in Castelnuovo as we had always done. My mind drifted to simpler times, before the war, when fear was not our constant companion.

I looked from my empty plate to the window. It was dusk already and the setting sun reflected a soft lavender hue in the eastern sky. I wondered why the clear sky had signs of lightning off in the distance. Then there was a flash across the valley, toward Barga. Seconds later I heard the explosion and I knew it wasn't a thunderstorm.

There was a great thudding crash and the ground trembled underfoot. The table shook and dishes rattled in the cupboard and thin streams of dust fell from the rafters overhead. Everyone around the table froze. I looked frantically from my mother to my brother and my sisters. Time seemed suspended. The entire household scrambled to the door.

Screams could be heard from the lower end of the village. Women and children were crying. Men's voices were shouting, "Where did it hit?"

"Run everyone, run into the village and take cover," came a neighbor's shout from above. I could hear shouts in German, too, coming from the direction of the blast below us.

"What's happening?" I cried.

"It's coming from Barga, so it must be the Allies bombing us," Cesar coughed through the dust. "They know the Germans are here."

"Cesar! Take care of your little sister!" my mother cried out behind me. I felt someone take hold of my arm and pull me toward the walkway by the side of the house.

"We need to move, Bruna. Run!" cried Cesar. "Our house faces Barga."

Cesar, Mery, and I ran up the walk from our house and into the village, followed by Aurelia and Pina who held Mamma between them. We ran instinctively into the piazza. Everyone else had the same idea. All our neighbors had also run to the center of the village.

"That sounded like it hit the vineyards right under your house," Alfezio said, as he hobbled over, out of breath. "I was at Evelina's, way up above. But the blast shook everything there just the same."

I saw the Germans leaving the houses and running toward the meadow.

"Follow them," cried Vincenzo. "Run where the soldiers are running. They're taking cover."

"Do you think there are more blasts coming?" Cesar asked, out of breath.

"Do you want to wait around to find out?" answered Dante as he grabbed Aurelia's hand and ran with her. People were beginning to move from the center of the village to the Bora valley behind it.

As people rushed toward the valley, we heard another boom. In the time it took me to realize that another bomb was on its way, it was already upon us. The sound was a shrill hum commanding quiet awe as it flew overhead. I saw the mortar shell make contact right near us. The ground shook again, sending waves of tremors underfoot.

The impact produced a deafening blast, hurling debris and chunks of brick wall everywhere. Centuries-old stone houses, lovingly constructed by our ancestors, became mounds of rubble. Pieces of glass and rocks became projectiles, raining onto the deserted piazza, followed by a billowing white cloud of choking dust. The structures that had sheltered us now pierced our skin and bones.

The cries and screams of children eclipsed the clunking sounds of rubble falling from the sky and onto the cobblestones. People threw themselves in doorways, under awnings and porticos to protect themselves from the mortar chunks.

As more blasts came, Cesar flung himself on top of me to keep me from being hit by flying debris. My ears rang from the explosions. I could barely hear the people around me coughing and sobbing. Cesar stirred and coughed. A cloud of dust had engulfed us.

"Cesar!" I gasped. "Cesar, are you hurt?"

"No," he sputtered and coughed again. "You?" He sat up slowly and checked my arms and legs for injuries.

"I think I'm all right." I shook my head to try to clear the ringing in my ears. "But what about Mamma? Where is she?"

"I'm here," Mamma called. She was sitting against the

side of a house with Mery and Pina. All were covered in dust. Alfezio was beside them, awkwardly positioned due to his missing leg. He was wiping his face with a handkerchief that looked as though it once might have been white.

"Is anyone hurt?" Mamma looked to those around her. There were a few scratches and cuts, but nothing serious. "Cesar," she croaked. "You must check on Nonna and Nonno."

"All right," he agreed. "Bruna, you stay with Mamma." He got up and turned around, but stood rooted to the spot as he faced the center of town. The devastation was horrific.

As the dust cleared the effects of the shelling was evident. Unfortunately, Alfezio saw it too. The impact had blown away the entire front of his beloved library, leaving a gaping hole in its wake. His cherished books were strewn about, charred and burning from the heat of the explosion. There was practically nothing left.

The grimace on Alfezio's face said everything. In a second, all that he had worked so hard to preserve was gone. "No," Alfezio cried. "Not my library." He had his handkerchief to his mouth, his hand in a fist. Awkwardly, he turned onto one hip to position himself so that he could get up from the ground. He had lost his cane in the mayhem.

"Alfezio," Mamma said, still on the ground. "Never mind that. You are unhurt. That's what matters."

"My books. They're gone." Anguished beyond consolation, he began hobbling over to the void that was once his home.

"Alfezio, let's go to the Bora. It'll be safer there," said Cesar starting after him.

"I'll go with you, Alfezio," I cried. I started to walk to him as he headed to the center of the piazza.

"My library," Alfezio despaired as he looked into the cavernous hole, a thin cloud of dust still hovering inside it. His hands were on his head, as he stood on the edge of the hole.

"No, Bruna!" Cesar grabbed my arm. "It's too open over there. You go with Mamma, I'll help him…" But Cesar didn't even have time to finish his sentence.

Silence hung in the air for a moment, and then there was another roar, once again from the eastern horizon. The people in the street had barely risen to their feet from the previous hit when they began screaming and running for cover once more.

"Get down! Get down!" yelled Cesar.

I threw myself down and crawled over to my mother as Cesar clambered over to a wall facing away from the hillside. I put my hands over my ears and counted to ten. And then, another blast. The ground shook and the air moved over us like a tidal wave. More rubble and pieces of sharp wooden shrapnel rained down on us, some piercing our skin.

I screamed and buried my head in my mother's lap. She covered my face with her arms. Pina was on the other side of Mery, covering her body with as much of her own as she could.

I remained burrowed in mother's lap, too frightened to lift my head to look. Around me were the sounds of muffled screams and cries. I wanted to stay here where I was, next to my mother forever. I felt hands on my shoulders, lifting me up by my dress fabric. Panic filled their eyes as Pina and Mery yelled at me.

"Move!" cried Pina. "We have to move now!"

Mery pulled my hands from my ears. "We have to get to Vincenzo's, now!" She forced me up as Pina helped mother to her feet.

"Cesar! Don't go over there! Come back," Mamma cried out. I looked over to see where he was.

"No, Bruna. Don't look there," said Mery through tears, turning me away.

"Why?" I asked. I felt an uneasy jolt in my stomach. "What is it?"

Chapter 21

The bomb poured hundreds of projectiles of wood and ancient building stones onto the few villagers remaining in the piazza. Through the dust, I could make out my brother's familiar figure huddled over a body. I saw that there was someone lying on the ground near what used to be Alfezio's library.

Cesar was only there for a moment, and then he came running back to us. As he approached, he wiped his eyes. "Down to Vincenzo's house, all of you," he said, an uncharacteristic mix of despair and anger in his voice. Cesar grasped mother and Mery's arms and Pina had me. The anguish on my brother's face was clear.

"Wait Cesar. Was that Alfezio?" I was incredulous. My

eyes stung and filled with tears. "He's hurt. We can't just leave him there."

"Alfezio is dead," Cesar gulped. He grasped my shoulders and held me at arm's length. "A piece of shrapnel pierced his skull. There's nothing more we can do for him."

"No!" I screamed.

"Bruna, just keep running."

We passed the familiar archway leading to our refuge. As we ran, we saw no one else, no villagers, no soldiers. Everyone was gone. An eerie quiet hung over the little town, like a stifling blanket. I heard a child crying in the meadow on the other side of Vincenzo's house. Then another boom from Barga. This time the bomb cut the air to the south. It hurtled by, making a high-pitched sound as it found its mark, finally making contact with one of the houses facing Barga in the upper village.

I ran ahead of Pina in a blind flight, and lost my footing on the steps descending to Vincenzo's house. I fell, sliding down the stairs on my back. I reached the safe house first, with Pina close behind. Cesar said nothing else. He kept low to the ground and pulled both my mother and sister until they reached shelter. He closed and secured the door. "Vincenzo! It's Cesar."

No one answered.

"Come," he said. "Get inside. They're in the back. Let's go." Cesar led us to the very back of the house to the isolated cold storage room dug into the hillside. He pulled on the latch but it was locked from the inside.

"It's us," Cesar said. "Open the door!"

"How many are you?" came a hesitant voice from inside.

Cesar didn't say a word. Instead, he pounded on the door so hard that the hinges creaked.

"Stop, Cesar," cried Mamma.

"It's Cesar! Let him in!" We heard Ersilia's voice from inside.

The door swung open to reveal a disheveled, terrified group of people — an assortment of villagers from different families, all hiding in the storage space that had become a bunker. They had come together in a moment of sheer panic and desperation. Ersilia and her sisters, Vincenzo and his family, and us. We silently huddled there in the cramped, musty sanctuary for the entire first night of the bombings. The distant sound of the artillery fire in Barga gave rise to the imminent high-pitched sound of the mortar shells soaring westerly overhead, one after the other. The Nazis now returned fire overhead with their gunners, relentlessly splitting the air. The sound of smashing buildings and roads was all around us.

"Why are they firing on us!" I shouted to my mother. "Aren't the Allies supposed to be helping us?"

"They're firing on the Nazis!" Cesar yelled above the shelling. "We are just in the way."

As the destruction raged above us, I could only think that every distant blast would be the last sound I would hear. If I didn't hear the screeching, then the bomb would already be upon us, and after that I would hear nothing else.

I looked around the makeshift shelter at the people around me and prayed that my grandparents were safe in their house.

Surely someone was able to get to them. I looked at my siblings and my mother, and hoped that we would all remain safe. I thought of Eleonora in Florence and of Alcide and I prayed that they were safe as well. Mercifully, the blasts finally stopped during the long night.

I had too much time to think that night. For the first time, I thought about my father and why he wasn't here to protect us. Even though we received occasional letters from him, I wondered why he had never come back to us, why he had stayed in Brazil. He should be the one helping Mamma instead of Cesar. He should be with us, fighting the enemy like my brothers, not safe in South America somewhere, so far away from danger. I was never allowed to talk of this to my mother, and when I asked my siblings they would tell me to be quiet. Sometimes I wondered why he never cared to meet me. That night, I hated him.

Chapter 22

In my dream I saw the outline of a man walking away from a bright light in the outlying background. He looked like my brother Alcide. He was tall and had the same gait. As he came closer, I felt joy. I wanted to go to him, but someone was pulling at my arm. Mamma was shaking me awake. The others were already on their feet, brushing off dust and soil from their clothing in a pointless effort to appear presentable.

"Is it over?" I murmured, still half asleep.

"It appears so, for now," said Mamma. "We need to get up and see what is left of the village."

We left the storage room and shuffled into the main house. Vincenzo's house had been spared, save for the dust and loose plaster on the floor. The group huddled around the door.

"Are you ready for this?" asked Vincenzo, his hand on the latch.

"What will we do if we're not?" replied Cesar. "Stay here forever?" He reached over Vincenzo's hand and unlatched the door, opening it slowly. It was barely dawn and all was quiet. A thin strip of pink appeared over top of the mountains on the horizon. I could hear distant coughing and crying. More muffled were the sounds of German voices because they were in the Bora behind the village, farthest away from the line of fire.

"Let's go," said Ersilia.

"No," said Cesar firmly. "You women stay here, out of sight. Vincenzo, you come with me."

I kept silent, and watched the men move out into the breaking dawn. The birds chirped their early morning songs, oblivious to the happenings of the night before. I wondered numbly if everyone but us had been killed last night. What if we were all that was left in our village? *No, that could not be.* We had all fought too hard to survive this far. It couldn't be over in one night!

"Bruna?"

I jumped, startled out of my daydream. "Mery! Oh, you scared me," I said clutching my chest.

"Come on. Wipe your face and eat something. There's some old polenta here." Mery handed me a napkin with the cornmeal. I couldn't even look at it.

"Eat, Bruna," Mamma insisted.

"How can you think of food now, Mamma? I feel sick to my stomach."

"I do, too. But if we don't keep up our strength, we are no good to anyone."

By the time we managed to put some food together, the men returned bearing relatively good news. "It appears as though Alfezio was the only one killed last night," reported Cesar. "We need to bury him. Father had him moved to the church rectory."

"Save for a few cuts and bruises, everyone is accounted for," Dante added. "But a lot of the houses were destroyed."

"Never mind the houses. Poor Alfezio," I sighed. "He was such a good man. Why him?"

"If I had the answer to that question…never mind. But, we do need to attend to Nonna's house," said Cesar. "Demetrio took them in."

"What should we do, Cesar, go back home or wait here?" asked Pina.

"We might as well go home. There is no telling when or if they'll start again. In the meantime, those villains in the Bora will order us back to work."

With that, we bid each other good-bye and made our way back to our respective houses, or what was left of them.

The devastation that I saw on my way home was more than I could bear. Dozens of houses had been damaged, especially those closest to the road facing Barga. Miraculously, Poggetti was untouched. The adjacent house, however, was not so lucky. Paolo and Alice's house had a gaping hole in the top floor from a mortar shell and Paolo was frantic. "Look at what those bastards did to my house!" Scores of townspeople were now without homes, in addition to those who were already displaced because of the occupying Germans.

Thankfully, the Nazis didn't round us up that morning to work. I guessed that they were probably regrouping. The villagers used this precious time to help the families devastated by the first round of shelling to gather whatever possessions they could salvage. I thought of Alfezio — a man who survived the Great War, only to die in desperation knowing that his one passion in life was to be no more.

Chapter 23

In the weeks that followed, the Allied bombings continued and became more vigorous and unrelenting. We often wondered whether the Allies knew the difference between Italian civilians and Nazi soldiers. The Nazis returned fire from the ground with their gunners and machine gun nests. We had to tread carefully during daylight as the shelling increased when the bombers saw activity on the ground. When we heard the shrill sound of bombs overhead, everyone would run for cover, but no one knew where to run — the bombs could fall anywhere.

As the mortar shells continued from the sky, the Germans held fast to their position in our village. On the ground, the soldiers kept us in line with their guns and bayonets. We tried to avoid them by keeping separate as much as possible. We did what they told us to do. Cesar was forced to work daily for the Nazi captors, digging and building. My sisters and I continued to work in the old osteria, preparing food and washing dirty clothes for the Nazis.

In the meantime, our elderly and sick got sicker without the benefit of medicine or doctors. Nonno wasn't able to eat anything now, save for a few drops of broth and he was wasting away before our eyes. Edo's father, Enrico, was in his last days and in great pain. The Nazis had closed the dirt road to Castelnuovo. It was the only accessible road in and out of Eglio.

Even within our village, it was hard to care for our sick because of the constant threat of shelling and the imposed curfew. We tried to visit Nonna and Nonno as often as we could, but it was always a risk. Those living on the outskirts of town were hard to get to and we had to be back inside our home by curfew.

Occasionally, Pina would fill some clay pots with leftover food from the osteria that the soldiers hadn't eaten and take it to our grandparents. This was very courageous. If she were caught or wasn't back by dusk, she could be severely punished.

One day after we were dismissed from our labor, Pina ran ahead with her clay pots to our grandparents' house. She was determined to get there as soon as possible. Mery, Mamma, and I followed. We took the ancient little walkway behind the church that nobody used. We clung to the vines and brambles as we walked, so that we wouldn't fall into the Bora. Finally, we reached the big house. Nonna and Nonno loved it when people called it "the big house," because it gave them a sense of pride to own one of the biggest houses in the village.

We let ourselves in through the side door, which opened directly into the sitting room. In the center was a generously sized dining table and beside it stood Nonna's beloved hutch in its place of honor. It was a pity that it was empty, its contents buried under the soil in the barn. The window coverings were drawn and the room was fairly dim. Nonna sat silently in her chair, her arms resting on the handmade doilies.

"Hello, Nonna," said Mamma. "How is Nonno?"

"I don't know how he is because he's not speaking to me." She sniffed haughtily and looked away into the shadows. Her tone was curt. My sister and I looked at each other. A sense of something *not right* pressed heavily on my chest.

"Nonna, where is Pina?" asked Mery.

"Upstairs," she replied flatly. Nonno stayed upstairs in bed.

The three of us stepped quietly through the sizeable kitchen. It was scrubbed clean and smelled of lye. On the plank table were two vessels of broth, untouched. Mamma drew aside the curtain that hid the staircase up to the bedrooms. The creaky steps announced our arrival.

"Who's there?" called Pina from upstairs.

"It's us," answered Mamma. We were almost at the top of the staircase.

A sob escaped her. "He's gone."

As we turned onto the hall to the master bedroom, we saw

Nonno lying under the white sheet in his and Nonna's bed. He was motionless and gray.

"He is done suffering," said Mamma, wiping the tears with her forearm.

I was devastated. My world would never be the same. Our treasured grandfather, was gone. We would never have any more of our animated discussions or our trips to Castelnuovo together. My heart was broken. I began to cry and didn't want to stop.

"Bruna," Mamma sniffled. "Come say a prayer. Then take the broth to Edo's house for Enrico. After that you will need to go home and make sure you get there before curfew."

I drew close to the body of my poor, dear nonno. Would he have had a better chance if there had been a doctor attending him? We would never know. I said my prayer and held his cold hand for a moment before creeping downstairs without a word to anyone. I wasn't just sad, I was angry at the world for taking away my grandfather. He had been like a father to me, taking the place of the father I never knew.

I grabbed the soup container and left, not acknowledging Nonna. How could she not realize that her husband was dead? Was her mind that broken?

I walked to the Guazzelli's house in a daze, using the back streets. It would soon be dusk, so I had to hurry. I pushed the door open. "Hello?" I said in a hushed tone.

"I'm coming," Edo said as he approached the entry. He was now a good-looking young man of nineteen though he seemed much older to me.

"Hi, Edo," I stood in the doorway with the vessel in my hand. "I brought you broth from my mother for your father. It's from the osteria."

"You managed to take some from those devils, did you?" He took a drag from his cigarette and leaned on the doorjamb.

"Don't talk of them that way. You never can tell who's listening." Awkwardly, I handed him the broth.

He ran his fingers through his hair. "Look, I'm sorry. I don't mean to be rude. It's just that father is really sick." He took the soup. "If only I could get him to a doctor or the hospital. He's suffering so much." He began to tear up.

"I know, Edo. My nonno died yesterday, I think. We only got to him this afternoon."

Edo took a drag from his cigarette. "I'm so sorry, Bruna."

"Me, too." I felt the sting of tears in my eyes again, but I fought them back. He turned to put the vessel on the tiny kitchen table. Their house was small and it housed five siblings and his parents.

"I hope Enrico gets better soon." I looked away, dabbing my eyes dry.

Edo nodded, but he didn't appear hopeful.

Chapter 24

We all helped to prepare our grandfather for his final days with us. We washed him and combed his thin hair. Cesar dressed him in his best suit and a few bunches of wildflowers were collected to adorn his bedroom. He was laid to rest in his bed and we arranged as many candles as we could find around him as he rested there in the house. There were no funeral homes in Eglio.

In the next two days, a steady stream of mourners came to call. They did the best they could under the circumstances to make life easier for our family. People brought whatever food they had.

On the morning of the funeral, Cesar was at the cemetery digging grandfather's final resting place. The shelling had been too severe the day before. Mother was upstairs and had watched and prayed over our loved one through the night, as was the custom. We girls were all gathered in my grandmother's sitting room when we heard sharp steps approaching our door. Suddenly it swung open and on the threshold stood the little German soldier who had smacked me on the head with his rifle. I cowered in fear beside my grandmother, who was totally oblivious to the entire situation.

"You, *pattat, pattat!*" he barked, his rifle pointed at us.

The soldiers were conducting more and more surprise raids in the homes, looking for food as they ran short themselves. There were limited convoys able to deliver supplies up from Castelnuovo.

"Please, leave us alone," Aurelia said bravely.

"*Pattat, now!*"

"We have no pattat!" Pina shouted back.

At this, he lost what was left of his temper and launched into a tirade in his native language that would have intimidated the bravest of souls. But Mery would not be browbeaten.

"Pattat, upstairs," she pointed to the stairs off the kitchen. "Go and check upstairs for your damned pattat, you milky-skinned bastard." The latter portion of the comment was uttered under her breath — and of course, he had not an inkling of what it meant.

The soldier reveled in his potato triumph and stomped through the kitchen. His heavy footsteps clomped on the steps. Step one, two, three, four, five- first landing- six, seven…all the way to fourteen. Mery got up suddenly.

"Mamma's up there alone." She scrambled to the stairs, silently crept up to the first landing and craned her head around so that she could see what he was doing. We listened. *Clomp, clomp*…then nothing. Then a slow scrape as he turned on his heel and came down again. Mery clambered back downstairs and took her original place as if she hadn't moved, her hand over her mouth.

A gentler, quieter step replaced the stomps. The soldier's feet finally appeared in our sightline almost on tiptoe as he descended the staircase. When he reached bottom his face was ashen and his eyes glossy. His rifle was slung over his shoulder and his hat was in his hand. He made no eye contact and did not speak as he approached the front door. Before he exited, he turned and bowed slightly toward my grandmother and quietly departed. Not another word was exchanged. We all sat in silence.

"Good for you, Mery," said Pina. "But don't ever do that again."

Mother rushed down the stairs. "What on Earth…? Has he gone?"

"What did he do?" I asked.

"He froze in mid-step when he saw Nonno lying there. Then he took off his hat and bowed his head, as if he were praying. I wouldn't have believed it if I hadn't seen it." How could a hard-nosed soldier be so affected by the sight of a dead man? We were all speechless pondering what had just happened.

"Who was that nice boy?" asked Nonna, at long last, breaking the silence. "So respectful." She smiled and shook her head.

Each of us turned to look at her, dumbfounded. Then the snickers came. The snickers turned to laughter, and then even Mamma couldn't control herself. The absurdity of my grandmother's comment and the innocence with which she expressed it washed away some of the gloom. We all had a hearty laugh at the expense of the potato soldier.

We did have potatoes — and they remained ours. They were covered carefully with a tarp and blankets under the bed where Nonno lay. Mamma always said that it was the little victories that counted. Our day ended with a hurried funeral in the church followed by the procession and burial of our grandfather in the village cemetery, dodging mortar shells all the way.

❧

Despite all the sadness and disruption around us, life continued in our village and people still found love. Aurelia and Dante shared their love in the form of a very simple wedding ceremony in the village chapel. Aurelia was pregnant and a village on the front lines was no place for a woman who would have a baby in a few short months. Dante thought that it would be best if they tried to get away, and stay in Cornola, a quiet village higher in the mountains that had not been occupied by the Nazis. They received permission for their move from the German officers and left shortly after the wedding ceremony. They departed on foot, and we would not see Aurelia again until the next spring.

Chapter 25

Early autumn came with a crispness in the air that usually meant it was harvest time. But there could be no such thing this year. Our fields and roads were littered with landmines and our men were building more bunkers.

On the Gothic front, the Allies were growing more frustrated. By November 1944, the war in Italy had reached a stalemate, partly because of heavy rains. The Allies weren't advancing any farther, and the Nazis continued their waiting game. Our willingness and strength to survive was tested daily as the bombarding continued.

One late afternoon that autumn, when the bombings had been particularly intense for a few days, my good friend

Armida and her family were caught off guard. They had been gathering some chestnuts for flour, but when they heard the shelling they ran into their barn, which was located some distance from their home in the lower part of the village. Since it was dusk and the curfew was on, they decided to stay in the barn for the night. The barn was made of thick oak logs so they believed that this was a solid shelter that would withstand the attacks. Eva, Armida, and Maria huddled together and fell asleep in the barn.

The mortar shells began to explode around them late in the night. One of the heavy shells landed on the roof and the heavy oak rafters gave way, splintered into a million pieces, and fell to the ground.

We too, were caught by the oncoming bombardments and couldn't make it to the other side of the village in time. Poggetti was not too far above the valley where their barn stood. That night, I heard Eva's screams. I will never forget her cries. It was an inhuman sound, primal and visceral. Screams from her mother and sister filled the quiet moments between the shelling. No one could reach them. We knew that something was horribly wrong, but we couldn't get to them. It was too dangerous to even think of venturing out into that madness. I put my hands over my ears to block the sounds.

Finally, when the bombardment stopped, some of the men scrambled down to the barn. I was too frightened and hid upstairs in my brother's bedroom. I couldn't bear to see what had happened to Armida and Eva.

Mamma came to find me the next morning. She was very

upset, but she tried to explain what had happened. Eva was directly underneath the girder that had been cut clean in half by the blast. She tried to scramble out of the way in time, but couldn't. The heavy beam fell to the ground and crushed both her legs above the knees. That was when poor Eva screamed in agony. Armida's foot was crushed by the same beam as she tried to clamber to safety, and Maria's hand was crushed by another. During the night, despite their own serious injuries, Eva's sister and mother tried to stop the bleeding by wrapping rags around Eva's legs as tourniquets. But the raging outside went on for a long time and she lost too much blood.

The men of the village carried her out and appealed to the soldiers for help. Surprisingly, they let them take her to the hospital in Castelnuovo, but that was over six miles (10 km). Her family and some of the men took turns carrying her on the back trails through Sassi and down the footpath. They made it as far as the Sanctuary of Our Lady of the Snow just north of Sassi. Eva had bled so much that she wasn't even conscious, her legs were barely attached. They never made it to the hospital. Her family wanted her home so that she could breathe her last there, instead of on the side of the road like an animal. Word came that she had died. Maria died not long after. Her hand was severely injured, but Mamma believed that she died of a broken heart because her daughter had been killed.

The memory of that night impacted me the most. I couldn't understand why some were spared and others were not. Even at such a young age, I knew I was one of the lucky ones. It was a strange thought for someone as young as I was.

Shortly after that horrible night, Enrico, Edo's father, passed away. Enrico had been the rock that held that family together and now he was dead. Edo told me years later that his father had died in his arms, gasping out his last breaths, leaving him in charge of a young family. He said that he had wept openly when his father died, not only to grieve his passing, but he also grieved for himself. Now that his father was dead, and his older brother Mario was missing on the Russian front, would he be strong enough to take charge and look after his younger siblings and his mother? He had no choice.

As the weather grew colder, my hatred for both the occupying soldiers and the Allies grew deeper. I hated the Allies for bombing us and murdering my friends and I reviled the Nazi soldiers because they were the cause for all this misery. They were all dream-takers, thieves of hope, and robbers of optimism.

Chapter 26

Don Turriani, our beloved parish priest, was one of the bravest men I ever knew. He gave to his parish willingly and always assisted his parishioners with whatever they needed. The true measure of his character would not be realized until one day in late November, when the cord of a field telephone belonging to the Officer's command post was found severed in a field outside the village.

The villagers were going about their work as usual, trying to stay out of trouble, as always. Suddenly, there was a commotion of angry German shouting coming from behind the Palazzo. People began to scatter. "Bruna, run away, hurry!" shouted my mother. She and I were on kitchen duty that day.

Frightened, I ran out behind the archway and down to

the stone stairs leading to the cobbled lane just outside of Vincenzo's house. We were staying there more often as it had become too dangerous to go back to Poggetti since it faced Barga where the bombs were coming from. I got far enough away so that I felt safe but could watch from the top of the stairs at the retaining wall.

As the shouts continued, I recognized the commander's voice. He was the angriest I had ever seen him. He pointed to a group of soldiers who began grabbing villagers, prodding them at gunpoint toward the retaining wall just under the churchyard. I wanted to run away, but I was frozen.

Next, I heard boots on the move, clomping over the stones. It sounded like they were behind the church. Then I heard shouts and shuffling, clicking rifles, moans and sobs.

"You! Here!" shouted the interpreter. "And you! All of you!"

People passed me in a panic. I felt someone grab my arm and pull me. I ran alongside them into the house across from Vincenzo's. Ersilia and her sister Rita had plucked me up as they ran by and pulled me to safety. Once the door was shut and bolted, I whispered, "Why are they shouting? What happened to make them so angry? And where's my mother?" I suddenly felt very alone, separated from my family.

"Your mother and some of the other women are hiding in the church," answered Rita, trembling.

"What do they want with us?" I whimpered.

"They think that one of us did something to one of the telephone wires they buried in the Bora. They worry that we are sympathetic to the partisans." She gasped out the last bit of information with a sob. "We ran because they were starting to round up some villagers."

"Rounding them up for what?" I asked, my whisper barely audible. I debated whether to unbolt the lock and run to look for my family. I was still close to the door.

"Come sit with me by the stove," Ersilia said in a kindly voice. "Don't worry about your mother. She is a very smart woman."

I decided to listen to Ersilia and sat beside her near the warm embers. Outside the entire village was suddenly quiet. For a torturous hour we waited. For what, I didn't know.

Finally, we heard footsteps from wooden shoes, not Nazi boots. We looked into the narrow street from the tiny window. Among others, I saw my mother, Cesar, Pina, and Mery. I scrambled to the door, almost falling to get to them. I unbolted the door and grabbed at the latch. "Thank God, you're all right!" I cried. I reached for Mamma and pulled her in. The rest followed.

"Was anyone hurt?" I searched their eyes for answers. They were stunned, unable to communicate. "What happened?"

Cesar secured the lock from the inside. They sat in silence near the hearth, my mother with tears in her eyes. Cesar lit a cigarette.

"God in heaven!" Rita looked from one to the other, her palms open ready to receive a response. "What did they do? Who did they shoot?" She clasped her palms together, as if in prayer.

When I heard those words, my heart sank. They were looking to punish us for the cut wire. I gasped at the thought that they had killed some of our people.

"They killed no one," Mamma said, expressionless.

"No one?" questioned Ersilia, her eyes wide.

"No," Mamma's head moved slowly from side to side.

"It was Don Turriani who saved us," said Cesar. "He wouldn't let them touch us." Rita sat gaping at him in disbelief.

"How? How did he manage..." I was motionless, astonished.

Mamma spoke. "They went into the fields, behind the church in the Bora. They were shouting that a telephone wire had been cut and they wanted to punish the villagers."

"The commander and his men wanted to set an example," said Pina. "They were going to shoot some of us for disrupting their communication line."

"That's when I ran away," I whispered.

Mamma nodded and breathed deeply. "Cesar was one of the men they captured." All of us were shocked at this.

"Don't worry. I'm fine," he said. His voice sounded brave, but his hands were trembling.

"I couldn't think of anything else to do," Mamma continued. "So I ran to the church to Don Turriani. I told him what they were about to do. He didn't hesitate for one moment." Now that some of the shock had worn off, Mamma began to cry. "Don Turriani ran from the church, straight into the valley. I followed him to the edge of the Bora, but was too frightened to go with him." At that moment I imagined our priest running to his people, his robes flying in the harsh November winds.

Cesar continued the story. "The commander was there and he was yelling at the people. They didn't know what he was saying to them — everyone was confused. They were just working there and then the next moment they were hit and pushed against the wall. Father walked straight to the Nazi commander, his hands in the air in surrender. He approached the commander slowly, talking very calmly. He placed himself right in front of us and begged the commander to have mercy. We were already lined against the wall. They came so close to doing it."

Mamma wept. "They were all crying and moaning, men and women alike, powerless."

Cesar looked at Mamma and then at us. "They were preparing to shoot us," he continued, "but Father wouldn't move. He talked quietly to the commander. All the while, the soldiers were waiting for the commander's order to shoot. Father swore to the commander that his people would have done no such thing, that we had cooperated with the soldiers all these long months. The cord might have accidentally been chewed by an animal or cut unknowingly by a spade or shovel. He said, 'I will vouch for my people. They did not do this.'

"The commander threatened him, saying that he would be shot too, but Father still didn't move. He fell to his knees in front of the commander and continued to plead for our lives. He said to shoot him instead, to make him the example and let his people go.

"It took a while, but the Nazi commander finally let us go. He told Father that if it happened again the entire village would be executed. Then he told all of us to get out of his sight before he changed his mind."

I just sat stone still throughout the story, feeling grateful to our priest for offering to sacrifice himself for his people, my brother included. "And then what?" I whispered.

"Father thanked him," added Pina. She wiped at her eyes. "Everyone scurried away after that."

"What about Father?" I asked.

"I think he may have gone back to the rectory to lie down," said Pina. "When it was over, I saw that his hands were shaking."

PART SIX

Nazi Defeat and Liberation
1945

In December 1944, the Allies took control of the city of Ravenna, northeast of Tuscany. In retaliation, the Axis planned a ground offensive in which they tried to recapture some of the land lost to the Allied forces in Tuscany. This resulted in renewed aggression in the valley and mountain areas around Eglio. Safely hidden in bunkers and in the villagers' homes, the Nazi soldiers stubbornly held their ground.

In other parts of Europe, the Russian army was advancing deeper into formerly Nazi-occupied territory. On January 27, 1945, the concentration camp at Auschwitz was liberated by Russian troops revealing to the world the horrible crimes against the Jewish people. On January 31, the Russian army crossed the Oder River into Germany, less than 50 miles (80 km) from Berlin. Soon the Allies bombed Germany on a massive scale.

Isolated from the rest of the world, the citizens of Eglio knew nothing of what was occurring around them. What they experienced were the bombings and gunfire by Allied strafing aircraft flying low. The villagers continued to be the moving targets of the automatic weapons mounted on the underside of these planes.

In the spring of 1945, an important breakthrough occurred on the Gothic Line. Beginning with the Po Valley Campaign in northern Italy, Allied forces captured Lombardy, a region in north-central Italy bordering Switzerland, and swept downward toward the mountains of the Garfagnana region. One by one, pockets of Nazi-occupied territory in Italy were overtaken. On April 24, 1945, the Allies surrounded the last of the Nazi armies, taking the German front near Bologna. The war in Italy had finally come to an end. The agonizing months of captivity and forced labor under the Nazis were soon to cease for the people of Eglio, in a way that they never dared to hope for.

Chapter 27

Not long after Christmas Day, 1944, there was a particularly horrific exchange of fire. My family and I huddled in the back room of Vincenzo's house while Allied planes launched mortar rounds. Nazi soldiers returned fire at the Allies and, again, we villagers were caught in the crossfire. The drone of airplane engines overhead warned us moments in advance of their approach. Our only defense was to run and hide as far from the outside world as we could get — anywhere but out in the open.

"Hurry! Get in! There's more gunfire coming!" Vincenzo's voice was sharp. It had to be, to be heard over the sounds of war outside his front door. Earthshaking crashes were all around us as mortar shell after mortar shell whistled its familiar arrival above us and found its target, bursting into the buildings and any reinforcements that were left. The Nazi gunners discharged steady rounds of thudding artillery fire.

We ran for our shelter in Vincenzo's house, the women farthest in at the safest point, the men in closer proximity to the front of the room. We huddled close to one another, against the dirt walls. Vincenzo lit a lantern and, to our surprise, we saw that in our midst was one of the German soldiers, the short potato soldier with the steely blue-gray eyes. But his eyes were not so steely now. Instead he had the look of a frightened child. He must have followed us into the shelter when he heard the shots, terrified like the rest of us. He shook in the corner like a scared rabbit, alone, powerless, and afraid. I should have felt vindicated that he felt a small portion of what I felt every day, but instead I felt pity. I wondered, could there be a human being beneath all that cruelty, afraid to die like the rest of us?

The candle's flame quivered wildly with each pounding contact from the shelling. We all worried that this night might be our last. I was sure that our luck had run its course. I wept.

My sister Pina was hunched beside me. She was crying, too. My brilliant sister, whom I always relied on for strength, was crying like a baby. Mery was on the other side of Mamma, and then there was Nonna. They held onto each other, with their faces buried in their arms. Cesar was with the men on the opposite side of the room, and his sweetheart, Ersilia, sat devotedly beside him.

The drone of plane engines and gunfire seemed unrelenting. Then, *smash!* There was an enormous thud. The sturdy house shook to its foundations. The door to the shelter blew open, and displaced air spewed hot embers from the point of contact. Before we could even react to the sound, the bomb had hit Vincenzo's house.

With instinct that I can only attribute to great courage and love, Pina threw herself on top of me, shielding me from the flying rubble that swept like a wave across the stone floor. It took a moment for us to realize that we were not dead. We looked up in a daze at the destruction, coughing and sputtering as the dust entered our lungs.

There in front of us was a bomb — intact and imbedded under the front entrance. Burrowed into the ground, unexploded, the metal shell had left a cavernous hole in its wake. Through the thick cloud of dust, we could make out fallen eves and debris covering the living room and kitchen. We all sat rooted to the spot, stunned, our mouths gaping at the instrument of death right in front of us.

Everyone I loved was in the shelter that day — my family and as many of our neighbors as could fit. And then there was the potato soldier. If the bomb had exploded, we all would have perished. What happened that day to save our skins, I will never know. Perhaps whoever had assembled it was having a bad day and hadn't put everything together correctly. Or maybe it had not hit at the correct angle. Maybe it was just a dud.

"All right everyone, just stay calm," Cesar breathed hard. He closed his eyes and his head hung back for a moment. "Don't make any sudden moves." His voice was a husky whisper. His remark was a bit laughable since there was shooting and shelling all around us. Our own sudden movement would not have made much difference to the bomb.

But there we sat, staring at it, as if even blinking the wrong way would set it off. We flinched at every round, at every mortar shell, at each gunner thump for the next hour or so, not daring to even speak. Our whimpering had stopped and raw fear took over. We felt that our survival depended on our intense focus on the bomb. Nothing else mattered. *Keep still and quiet.*

When the shelling and gunfire finally subsided, Vincenzo made the first move. He got up cautiously, nodding toward Cesar and the other men. It was time to leave the shelter. The men held out their hands, the soldier included, helping the women up with unparalleled calm. One by one, we trod at a snail's pace, our backs against the walls using measured steps around the rubble and debris. With painstaking care, we all managed to step around the bomb giving it a wide berth. I lost track of where the potato soldier went. Instead I watched the faint pink sun sinking slowly into the western horizon.

We scrambled to the back trails around the village, and then ran to the closest safe house, paying no heed to the dangers surrounding us.

Elsewhere in the village that day, there was severe damage to many other homes, including my grandparents' house. A bomb penetrated the roof and traveled through the upstairs and the living room, ultimately coming to rest in the crawlspace in the basement. It too, remained there, unexploded, until it was extracted after the end of the war.

Chapter 28

I have heard it said that those of us who lived and survived World War II were ordinary people living in extraordinary times. Of this I'm certain. I do believe that, despite all that we suffered, we were among the fortunate people. I can't begin to understand what others in concentration camps suffered, those who were starved, tortured, and mercilessly gassed and murdered. The only thing I can speak to is what I and my family suffered to survive.

The Allies (mainly U.S. and Indian forces), lost much of Northern Tuscany that December, but not for long. By January 1945, Allied forces had regained control and then everything seemed to grind to a halt for us. The remaining winter months brought relative quiet to our village, save for the usual oppressive shadow of the Nazis. There was a stalemate in the valley, with neither side able to advance successfully. But elsewhere in the world there was a definite turn in the tide. The Nazis' days were numbered. We didn't know it at the time, but soon they would be gone.

By April 1945, we were all listless and tired from the years of war. Our captors were distracted, anxious, almost preoccupied. Most of our houses had been destroyed. The majority of the dwellings that faced the Garfagnana valley had gaping holes from the constant barrage of mortar shells. The insides of the houses were exposed, the contents spilling out like the guts of a wounded animal. In the interior of the town, many homes suffered the same fate, either destroyed by Allied aircraft bombings or mortar attacks. Their inhabitants crowded together and stayed with other families that still had intact homes. We stayed with any family that welcomed us, sometimes sheltered in the chestnut dryers and barns in the fields behind Eglio, depending on where we found ourselves during an attack.

When the Nazi front fell in Bologna, I believe that the German soldiers in our village had been given instructions to defend their post, to stay in Eglio until their dying breath. But this is not what happened.

Instead, one morning we awoke to an unusual quiet — peaceful, hushed tranquility. Gone was the shouting, the clicking of boots on the stones, the harsh commands. We poked our heads out of our makeshift shelters, like gophers waking from a long sleep to see what had happened on the outside. All was abandoned and silent. No one was skulking around with a gun, ready to shoot if we ventured out of line. We left our houses, shelters, and barns in search of our oppressors.

Our people stepped gingerly out into the village, slowly, warily. There was equipment here and there, where it had been left the night before. The men went to look in the windows of the houses typically used by the officers. No one there. We searched the bunker and the officers' eating areas. No Nazi soldiers. The men searched the houses still standing and found only leftover equipment. No arms. Was this all a trick? Were they testing us? Or had they just disappeared into the woods in the night like common thieves?

"The Palazzo," said Oreste, his eyes wide with hope. Would the wireless radio still be there? A contingent of men scurried to the big building and cautiously entered. There it was on the table in the kitchen. They turned it on, but only static could be heard.

The news came to us in piecemeal fashion. The Nazi forces had been pushed out of Garfagnana, but small battles were still being fought. The Allied forces and the Italian partisans scoured the mountains, looking for remaining Nazi soldiers and fascist sympathizers, and searching for any hidden arms.

A few days later, a disguised Benito Mussolini was captured in northern Italy trying to escape. He was shot and hanged in Milan by the partigiani the next day. He and his mistress were hung upside down in a public place for all to see, confirmation to the Italian population and to the world of his execution. Other members of his puppet government were also put to death by the Italian partisans, and their bodies put on display.

Within days, the American Allies approached Eglio to liberate us and secure their position. They carefully made their way from Castelnuovo on the other side of Sassi, where it was safe. I remember being frightened at seeing soldiers again, although these soldiers looked very different from the Nazis. They carried rifles, but the Americans appeared more relaxed and friendly. Were these the same men who had pummeled us with mortar shells all these months? I was afraid of them at first because of this, but my brother explained to me that they were simply trying to destroy the Nazi oppressors. As they walked into our village, our liberators talked with the villagers through an interpreter. To our surprise, there were even a few who spoke a bit of Italian, their families having immigrated from Italy to America.

The *Americani* and our men discussed what had occurred in Eglio for so many months, what the Nazis had done in our village, and where their arms might be. Cesar, Vincenzo, Oreste, and other villagers answered their questions honestly and freely, giving them any information that might be of strategic significance. The Americans listened attentively and seemed sympathetic to the dangers we had been through. They understood that we had been used as human shields by the Nazis.

The men of Eglio invited the liberators into Ferrari's bar and poured them drinks from wine that had been hidden all these months. They drank a cin cin toast to the disappearance of our captors and to the liberation of Italy. Whatever food the women could find was brought and shared with the victors. The men clapped their newly found American soldier friends on the back. They ate and drank with them for a while and even sang songs. There was joy once more in Eglio. Laughter could be heard in the street and celebration was in the air.

The Americans continued through Eglio, up into other villages higher in the mountains. Later they cleared the land-mines and allowed our men to dismantle the barbed wire fences as they went. Eventually, we heard radio broadcasts of Nazi Germany's surrender and of Hitler's cowardly suicide. It was May 1945, and at last, the war was over!

Chapter 29

Celebrations, though long awaited, were bittersweet for most of us. There were many in our village who had lost loved ones in the terrible years of Italy's war. Just about every family in Eglio had lost a son or daughter, husband, mother, or father.

Some of our men who had served in the military, began trickling into town shortly after the peace declaration to the great delight of their families. But others were never heard from again, their bodies buried in some obscure battlefield in Eastern Europe or in a mass grave in a prisoner of war camp. Edo's brother, Mario Guazzelli, for example, never returned from the Russian front. There was also the tragedy of the villagers who had lost their lives in Eglio, such as Alfezio, Eva,

Enrico, and my nonno. They were no longer here to celebrate the end of the war.

But life resumed for those of us who were left alive. The roads were cleared of landmines with great efficiency and people started to venture out again. Aurelia and Dante came back to Eglio with a beautiful baby boy. Cesar and Ersilia were married. Armida, Beppina, and I renewed our friendship after months of virtual imprisonment within our own community. And Edo did manage to become the man of the family for his mother and three siblings with some initial assistance from our kind and brave priest Don Turriani.

Our family was one of the more fortunate ones. We were able to move back home to Poggetti. Though there was damage to the upper level of the house from the shelling, it was repairable.

We were grateful to have Cesar with us. But the war was over and we had not heard from Alcide for years. There was no word of his whereabouts and we had to assume that he had been killed or captured by the Nazis. Our dear Alcide, tall and imposing, fearful but brave, another casualty of war. Mamma tried to accept that her son was gone. I, on the other hand, still believed in miracles. And miracles often come when one least expects them.

co

It was October 1945, and slowly life was becoming normal again. Death had come to claim our nonna who had just passed away and we were still mourning her. Remarkably, she had made it through the war unscathed. But a few months later, she had surrendered to her many frailties, dementia being only one of them. Earlier that same day, Mamma, Mery, and Eleonora, who had come back to Eglio for the funeral, and I had gone to Nonno's big house to clear out her belongings. It was not a difficult task as many of her things were still buried in the barn, still too dangerous to approach because of the landmines that might be buried there.

The morning after Nonna's funeral, I poked my head out of the window at Poggetti and breathed in the clean, crisp morning air. The fog was over Barga down in the valley, covering it like a tufted cotton blanket. But we mountain folk already knew that this was going to be a beautiful day.

I strode downstairs and washed, combed, and braided my hair, securing the strands at the bottom with a ribbon. Mery, Nora, Cesar, and Mamma were already at breakfast when I joined them. Mamma had fixed porridge, thick and sweet with honey and milk. The coffee was steaming hot and smelled heavenly. Just as we were done and starting to clear the table, we suddenly heard a commotion echoing off the hills opposite the valley. Children were shouting, not frightened shouts, but excited, happy cries.

"Matilde!" came a shout in the distance, echoing in the valley. "Matilde, come quickly!"

Mamma was at the sink. She stopped scrubbing the plate

in her hand and angled her ear to the window. Mery came closer to the door and stood, waiting. I hurried outside to the railing to see what could be causing such a fuss.

"It's Alcide!" they yelled. The faint children's voices were coming from around the bend north of the village, towards Sassi.

Cesar got up from his seat and dashed to the railing. He leaned over the barrier to listen.

Then more shouts. "Matilde! It's Alcide!" The voice was closer now. "Alcide is coming!"

"He's back! He's walking up from Castelnuovo!" said another voice.

"Cesar?" Mery looked at our brother. I looked at Mamma, her face framed through the kitchen window. Her expression was frozen. I ran inside and grabbed both her hands in mine. "Mamma, did you hear?" She nodded her head.

"Could it be?" The wrinkles on her forehead crinkled as her appearance took on an ashen gray color. Her lip was trembling.

"Matilde! Cesar!" This time they were calling from the road underneath our house. I ran back outside with Eleonora in tow. We stood beside Cesar, looking down at a small contingent of children on the road below. "We saw him! He's coming! Alcide has come home!"

"Where is he?" shouted Cesar. The children babbled and yelped altogether and pointed towards Sassi.

This was too much for mother. I turned to see her faint, crumpling in the kitchen like a rag doll. Mery ran to her and grasped her under the arm, pulling her gently onto a nearby chair. At once, I dashed to Mamma's side and held her hand as I crouched beside her.

Cesar stuck his head in the door. "You take care of Mamma. I'm going to find Alcide!" He barely got the words out and he was gone, shouting at the children below to take him to Alcide.

"I'm going, too. I need to see this for myself." Eleonora tore out after him, giddy with excitement.

Mery looked at me and then stood up tall. "Bruna, you stay here with Mamma." In an instant she was gone, too.

I was alone with Mamma. My mind was racing. I had to wake her and *quickly*. She had to be ready for Alcide when he came back home! I wrung out a clean cloth in cool water and placed it on Mamma's forehead. I heard people shouting and cheering in the village.

"Mamma?" I gently tapped her hand. "Wake up." I flipped the cloth over her forehead. "Alcide promised you that he would be back and he has kept his promise."

Chapter 30

Slowly Mamma began to awaken. Her eyes opened. She glanced around the room at first and then down at me. Tears brimmed in her eyes.

"Heavenly Father," she cried. "God has heard our prayers." Her hands drew mine to her lips and she kissed them. As she did that, I sensed a shadow at the door. I turned, and it was Alcide. He was very thin and looked so much older than when he left. But it was Alcide — a big, familiar boyish smile on his face. He had been gone for four years.

"Alcide!" My mother stood to run to him. He stretched out his arms and, in two of his great strides, he lifted her up in a huge hug.

"Mamma!" he wept. There was no more to say. I was

weeping too, as I held on to both of them. Cesar stood at the door and cried, his tough exterior reduced to tears of joy. Mery and Eleonora joined our embrace. Pina and Aurelia, who had been in the village when they heard the commotion, had met him earlier and accompanied him to Poggetti for our reunion, were inside the kitchen now, too.

"You should have seen everyone out there," Cesar stifled a sob as he spoke.

"Dozens of villagers followed Alcide into Eglio from Sassi. It was like a parade, children and adults, all cheering him on."

"When he walked into Eglio, people thought they were seeing a ghost," Eleonora explained.

After our long embrace, Mamma held Alcide at arm's length and looked up at his weathered face. Her eyes were radiant, more radiant than I had seen them in years. "Alcide. It is you. Thank the Lord, you've come home."

"Yes, it is me," said my big, tall brother. "I'm so relieved to be home. You don't know what I went through to get back here."

Mamma gave him another great hug. "Look at you. You are all skin and bones." She held his face in her hands. "I'll get you something to eat!"

"Alcide," I was the first one to ask, "where have you been all this time?"

He looked down at me and with a huge smile he responded. "I will tell you everything, young lady, but right now I am very hungry."

❧

Alcide's eyes looked far away, farther than the remote mountain peaks of San Pellegrino. He had eaten his fill and now he just breathed and looked lovingly around our tiny kitchen. He smiled at my mother as she held his hand. Cesar offered him a cigarette, which he took obligingly. He took a long puff and then with a ghostly quality in his eyes, he began his story.

"I was in Rhodes in the Aegean Sea, serving in the Italian infantry. My work was mostly patrolling the border. Then in 1943, when the Italian government fell, the Nazis took control of Rhodes, the biggest of the Aegean Islands. All the Italian soldiers stationed there were arrested. Most had wanted to change sides and fight with the Allies.

"First we were put on a ship bound for Turkey. In Turkey, we were eventually made to board a train, where we were to be taken to a prisoner of war camp. A handful of us soldiers managed to escape by breaking open the lock on the train car. It was the dead of night and we jumped off the moving train down an embankment. Rapid gunfire followed us, so we lay down flat on the field beside the tracks, praying they would miss. Though I lay as flat as I could, they managed to graze me in the backside. The gunshots bored holes in my pants."

He laughed at this, while I listened, horrified. "Where were you when you jumped off the train?" I asked.

"We had no idea where we were. All we knew was that we were escaped prisoners of war with no intention of returning to fight for the Fascists.

"Little by little, our group thinned out. Those of us who were left traveled covertly through the mountains, out of sight from the battles around us. We worked in hiding, in Bulgaria for sheepherders and farmers for the rest of the winter. While we waited for spring, we tended to the sheep, labored on the farms and in turn the farmers fed us, clothed us, and allowed us to sleep in their barns.

"The following spring I started my long journey home again, heading northwest into Yugoslavia, crossing the frontiers over the mountains. After months of traveling, I finally crossed the border from Yugoslavia into northeastern Italy. This was the summer after the collapse of the Fascist regime in Europe. I kept going southwest, on foot over the Alps, through villages, dodging minefields and barbed wire fences. The autumn after the end of the war, I walked south through northern Tuscany. By the time I finished, I was exhausted and starving."

"What a horrifying experience," Nora interrupted. "You must have felt so alone."

Alcide nodded and continued. "Yesterday, I finally made it into Castelnuovo where people knew me. They fed me and gave me a place to stay for the night and clean clothes. They wanted me to stay longer, but I couldn't. I needed to get home. So this morning I set off for Eglio. I climbed the last of the steep hills up to my beautiful mountain village and to my family." His eyes welled up with tears. "I hoped that I would find you all as I had left you. I heard of the Nazi presence in Garfagnana. I prayed that you were all unharmed."

"Oh, Alcide, Mamma never gave up hope," Pina said, her eyes welling up again. "For us it is as though you have risen from the dead."

"And for me," said Alcide. "It is like coming back to life."

"For our family," I added, "it is a new beginning."

I was grateful that our little family was reunited. We had outlived the war. It was, at long last, the end of a fearsome upheaval. We had made it through the hard times, thanks to our own resilience and the strength of our mother who had been our rock throughout our lives.

Later that week, I was cleaning out one of my nonna's dresser drawers, when I discovered an old photo. I recognized the face instantly. It was a photograph of her son, my father, as a young man. After the war, we had begun to receive regular mail from him again. Though he sent us money from time to time, he had no desire to return to us.

Perhaps it was because I was getting older or perhaps it was because of all we had experienced in the last few years of war, but I suddenly saw my mother in a new light. Her dignity and quiet grace had held our family together through very difficult years. She had supported and raised all of us, alone. During the war, she had kept us together as best she could, always including her husband's parents, my nonno and nonna, as part of our family. I was so proud of her and admired her to the deepest measure, not only because she was my mother, but also because she was a woman of great courage and resolve.

I didn't know what my life's journey or my future held in store. But I did know one thing. I could draw strength from my friends, my family, and especially from my mamma, for whatever life would bring to me.

When war came to Eglio, all I could see was the hardship and brutality, the desolation and unfairness. But in the end, our wartime experiences left me with a deep appreciation and understanding of life — an appreciation of every moment that we have to share with the people we love. Perhaps some day, my own children will pass my experiences on to their children, so that they, too, will hear the story of war in my town.

Author's Note

When I interviewed Bruna, my mother, during the writing of this book, she became tearful many times. I could sense that recalling these events still evoked anxiety in her after all these years. I don't believe that one ever recovers from such traumatic events. One merely learns to live with the physical and emotional scars. Yet, despite the horror experienced by my family, they did go on to live successful and happy lives.

Bruna did marry Edo. They had my brother, after which they immigrated to Canada. Soon afterwards I was born to Bruna and Edo. My beautiful aunt Mery wed Guido, the young man from Eglio, and they had two equally beautiful daughters. They moved to Canada before my parents did. Aurelia and Dante moved to Pisa where Dante became a *carabiniere,* a policeman, and eventually a detective. They were blessed with two boys. Cesar and Ersilia had a son and moved to Val d'Aosta, where Cesar worked after the war blasting and building tunnels. Alcide married Zelinda, and he became a *corazziere,* a special guard to the Italian President. They moved to Rome and had two children. Eleonora married Mario from Florence. They had no children but owned and ran a successful hotel near Florence, where my mother worked soon after the war. Pina worked away from Eglio for a time but eventually returned to take care of my grandmother, Bruna's mamma, Matilde. Pina never married.

As for Aurelio, Bruna's father, he never returned to Italy, and though he corresponded regularly with his family and helped to support them, he and his youngest daughter, the heroine of this story, never met.

My mother's battle with Alzheimer's Disease inspired me to record this little piece of history for future generations. I hope it inspires you, the reader. These stories of a long-ago war are a testimony to human resilience and the will to survive in the face of extraordinary times — the triumph of the human spirit over terrible adversity that most of us can only imagine. This story is a tribute to everyone in the village of Eglio, those who died and those who survived the Gothic Line occupation.

—E. Graziani

Bruna Pucci, the author's mother, at 17.

Edo Guazzelli, the author's father, went for military training, but never engaged in battle.

Matilde Lenzarini, Bruna's mother, married Aurelio Pucci who later worked in Brazil.

Bruna's sister Eleanora (seated at left in her nurse's uniform) worked at an orphanage in Florence during the war. When she sent this photo home she wrote on the back: "Don't look at me because I look funny — look instead at my babies."

Alcide was Bruna's youngest brother. He was selected to be a member of the Presidential Special Guard.

Bruna's big brother Cesar gave her away at her wedding.

Bruna and Edo posed with family and friends on their wedding day, August 16, 1952.

Eglio overlooks the Bora Valley, where villagers hid from gunfire and where the Nazis had built bunkers. Below the church (at right) is the wall where citizens were lined up to be shot before the town's priest saved them.

Acknowledgments

Thank you to Second Story Press for giving this true story a chance to be heard. To Carolyn Jackson for finding it, to Margie Wolfe for believing in its importance and helping it come to life, and to Sarah Swartz, for making it better.

Thank you to my brother, Enrico, and cousins, in Canada and Italy, for their support and good wishes.

About the Author

E. Graziani is a teacher and self-proclaimed life-long learner who believes in constantly setting new goals for herself and working hard to achieve them. Her love of history, word artistry, and storytelling help to fuel these goals as do her students who particularly enjoy her classroom read alouds. She has worked with the Alzheimer Society of Canada to raise awareness and educate people regarding this disease. She resides in Stoney Creek, Ontario, with her husband and four daughters. Other books by E. Graziani — *Alice of the Rocks* and *Jess Under Pressure*.